M000119878

SEARCH ENGINE
DOMINATION

The Proven Plan, Best Practice Processes & Super
Moves to Make Millions with Online Marketing

Contents

Contents

Search Engine Domination:
The Proven Plan, Best Practice Processes, and Super Moves to Make Millions Online

ISBN 978-0-9998649-5-1 Copyright © 2019 by Clay Clark and Clay Clark Publishing 1100 Suite #100 Riverwalk Terrace Jenks, OK 74037. Most often, printed in the United States of America, however we would be excited if a few copies were ever printed in Canada, Puerto Rico, or even on another planet. I would become upset if copies of this book were someday printed in China. All rights reserved. No part of this book may be used or reproduced in any manner whatsoever without written permission except in the case of brief quotations embodied in critical articles, or books and reviews. For additional information, address Clay Clark Publishing, 1100 Riverwalk Terrace #100, Jenks, OK, 74037. Clay Clark publishing books may be purchased for educational, business or sales promotional use. As of the time of the printing of this book, Clay Clark has 13 cats and hundreds of trees. For more information, please email the Special Markets Department at info@ThrivetimeShow.com. For a good time visit ThrivetimeShow.com, Patriots.com, or Cleveland-Browns.com.

"I'm dedicating this book to my beautiful and brilliant wife of 18 years. I appreciate you (Vanessa) for playing defense (managing the accounting and legal aspects of our businesses) so that I can focus nearly 100% of my time to playing offense (vision setting, content creation, marketing, sales, system building, etc.). Together, you and I make a GREAT team. Thank you to Jonathan Kelly for being the most effective and most loyal manager that the world has ever known. I love you both because of the people that you choose to be on a daily basis, and your relentless diligence."

CLAY CLARK

(Former U.S. Small Business Administration Entrepreneur of the year, founder of DJConnection.com, Co-founder of EpicPhotos. com, Co-founder of EITRLounge.com, etc..)

"I am dedicating this book to my wife, Stephanie Kelly who is the most amazing wife and mother on the planet, my daughter, Harper, the best dog in the whole world, Chauncey. Also, thanks to Darlon Tucker, and Devin Woolery for all of your hard work.

JONATHAN KELLY

(Clay Clark's business partner, Forbes.com contributor, and President of MYLEAgency.com)

Quick Note: "I want to thank Devin Woolery and Darlon Tucker 2% more than Jonathan Kelly" **- Clay Clark**

THIS BOOK WAS WRITTEN FOR THE GRINDERS, AND THE DILIGENT DOERS LIKE YOU WHO ARE WILLING TO PUT IN THE WORK.

"Do your home work and know your business better than anyone otherwise someone who knows more and works harder will kick your a$@."

- MARK CUBAN

(The iconic self-made billionaire, owner of the Dallas Mavericks and star of the hit TV Show, Shark Tank)

"Vision without execution is hallucination."

- THOMAS EDISON

(The man who is credited with inventing the first modern light bulb, recorded sound and recorded audio and he was the founder of General Electric)

"YOUR SUCCESS IS GUARANTEED WHEN YOU IMPLEMENT OUR PROVEN SYSTEM" - Clay Clark

Facts and Case Studies from Diligent Doers Like YOU:

"Clay and his team will give you the simple systems that people can work with on a daily basis and that simplicity brings POWER with it. So it shocked me how simple some of the stuff is. And at times, I am like...Why didn't I think of that and it's helped our church so much and after 6 months I can already see our trajectory going up. People are finding out about us, our number of new visitors is going up and I can see the marketing working."

- PASTOR BRIAN GIBSON

(Senior pastor of HisChurch.CC with locations in Amarillo, Texas and Owensboro, Kentucky)

"We've grown our business by 300% within 11 months. I would highly recommend Clay's systems to any entrepreneur or small business out there that is looking to take their business to the next level."

- TYLER AND RACHEL HASTINGS

(The founders of DelrichtResearch.com
- New Orleans, Louisiana)

"Last year sales this week was a mere $4,711.73 and the same year this week was $11,313.50."

- KAT GRAHAM

(Co-founder of BarbeeCookies.com
- Tulsa, Oklahoma)

"We've been using Clay Clark's systems since April of 2017 and have grown exponentially since that time. We have set up systems within the business that make my life much easier and we are also seeing the financial rewards of that. We went from owning 3 locations in 2016 to now we are up at 8 locations and we are still growing. The training that we have been getting from Clay is invaluable and we hope to keep growing with Clay's help."

- JENNIFER ALLEN

(Co-founder of BodyCentralPT.net
- Tucson, Arizona)

"The number of new customers that we have is up 411% within just the past year. We went from being virtually non-existent to the top page of Google and our competition Orkin and Terminix are massive companies."

- JENNIFER AND JARED JOHNSON

(The founders of Platinum-PestControl.com - Tulsa, Oklahoma)

"Within 4 months of implementing the system, our ophthalmology practice is up nearly 20% over last year. We are up between $30,000 - $50,000 each month of profits ."

- DOCTOR TIMOTHY JOHNSON

(Head of TuscaloosaOphthalmology.com
- Tuscaloosa, Alabama)

"We just set a record for the biggest January we've ever had. We are up 59% over last year. We've doubled our incoming leads. We've set records for the best day, the best week and the best month. And that is what has happened. It's working! Our team is more engaged and we have more sales!"

- CHRIS DEJESUS

(The founder of BreakOutCreativeCompany.com
- Poway, California)

"My sales are up from $60,667 in sales last May to $102,837 this year in May. BOOM! Out of the weeds onto the pavement."

- ROY COGGESHALL

(Owner and Founder of RCAutoSpecialist.com and TheGarageBA.com - Tulsa, Oklahoma)

"We've had record production during the past few months!"

- BRONSON SCHUBERT

(State Farm insurance agent -
Oklahoma City, Oklahoma)

"I had the pleasure of working with Mr. Clark in 2010 when I managed over 2.2 million square feet of downtown office and retail space. I can recommend him highly and without reservation. I had hired Mr. Clark to rebrand the portfolio, and to reach out to prospective tenants. Throughout the course of the campaign, Mr. Clark was a consummate professional. He conducted market research, built a web-site, and coordinated obtaining pictures, print materials, and gaining media attention within what I would deem record time. Within the first week of Mr. Clark going public with the campaign, he generated hundreds of prospective tenants. Mr. Clark's positive attitude is contagious, he is a hard worker, and he is genuinely a great guy to work with. I hope that in the near future I will have the opportunity to work with Mr. Clark again."

- DAVID ATKINSON

(The former Vice President of KanbarProperties.com - Owned by Maurice Kanbar (the prolific inventor, and the founder of Skyy Vodka) based in San Francisco, California)

"We've grown from 1 location to 10 locations in the past year."

- RYAN AND RACHEL WIMPEY

(Founders of TipTopK9.com, which now have locations in Boise, Idaho, Southlake, Texas, Oklahoma City, Oklahoma, etc.)

"Clay's helped us A LOT with our website. SEO is a thing that I thought was kind of joke or something that only your Apples of the world and Amazons could get to the top of the search results. But Clay said no, do these things and follow these steps. And I think now we are #2 for "Dallas Real Estate Photography" in Dallas. I would say that there is nobody out there that is a not a good candidate for the system. Today we are doing over $100,000 per month in sales. If you follow his systems and his tools, it works. Clay Clark is the way to go!"

- THOMAS CROSSEN

(The founder of FullPackageMedia.com)

"Clay's systems have been a game-changer for us. More sales, more attendance, more successes in business with a record year last season."

- TAYLOR HALL

(General Manager of the TulsaOilers.com professional minor league hockey team - Tulsa, Oklahoma)

"I heard about Clay on an article on Forbes.com. I think that because we have weekly phone call meetings it helps me to stay on track and have a clear idea on where I'm going. Every week I have homework and I have definitely become more proactive. It's amazing and it's keeping me accountable. It's hard to describe. It's just been ONE OF THE MOST AMAZING things I've ever experienced. Everything is very good and very practical."

- NICOLE SHIH

(Founder of Nestvy.com and assisted living placement expert - San Francisco, California)

"(Within 2 months) my closing percentage of success on calls is drastically improving by using humor (4 new contracts with 5 calls). We've increased our profits by $2,800 per week (12K per month of gross income). We are above 1,100 staffing hours, we had been stuck at 700. The procedures make me feel better."

CORY MINTER

(President of TrinityEmployment.com - Tulsa, Oklahoma)

"We are already ranking for the top of Google for a few keywords which is ahead of schedule."

- JOSH SPURRELL

(CPA and the founder of the Canadian accounting practice Spurrell.CA)

"You certainly were the on-site leader that we needed for this campaign. By watching you work with these students and seeing the result, I became reassured that hiring you to do exactly what you did was the right thing to do. Your team brought in over $120K in gifts and pledges, which may be an all-time ORU record! But I'll have more for you later. Again, thanks for everything....and don't drink too much Red Bull!"

- JESSE D. PISORS, B.A.

(1996) M.A. (2005) (Director of Alumni & Ministerial Relations | ORU.edu - Tulsa, Oklahoma)

"Hey Clay, Thanks for all your help last year, we've done a lot of work, reading and investing and the results are truly amazing. We now have our best staff ever, continuous increases and overall happiness like never before, and yes more profitable than in years and in a down economy)! I feel like we now have entirely new understanding on the importance of culture in the workplace."

- DAVE BAUER

(Maytag University Conference Attendee and the founder of ApplianceSolutionsTulsa.com - Tulsa Oklahoma)

"Within a month of listening to this guy, I've determined that I had to be a client of this guy. I now have a world-class website that creates leads and that is a huge win. I've experienced huge WINS and I've only been working with them for the past 3 months."

- MIKE SOMMER

(The founder of HickoryCreekInc.com Oconomowoc, Wisconsin)

"You single handedly saved this event for my dad (Tulsa Sports Charity Hall of Fame Basketball Hall of Fame induction ceremony for former Oklahoma State Basketball Coach, Coach Eddie Sutton). I think we are now drinking from your Kool Aid!!!"

- STEPHEN E. SUTTON

(Vice President | Former Public Sector / Financial Associations Portfolio Manager for SpiritBank.com - Tulsa, Oklahoma)

"I just want to let you know that I have just had a tremendous response to all of the things that you have helped me implement and just all the magic you have worked. Things are really picking up and I am just super excited that I have found you guys."

- SHANNON ROBERTS

(Founder of LoftyBeautyLounge.com - Jacksonville, Oregon)

"Last August we had 114 new patients compared to this August where we've had 180 patients. The system works."

- DOCTOR APRIL LAI

(Co-owner of MLKDentistry.com)

"They took over our marketing account a little over a month ago and it has been OVERWHELMING the response than we have had!"

- BRIDGETT HUNT

(Co-owner of RescueHeatAndAir.com)

"We own several fitness centers located in Topeka, Kansas, Joplin, Missouri and Bartlesville, Oklahoma. They create systems that are easier for your company to help you to duplicate and grow. I like Clay he makes everything entertaining and fun and he delivers the content in a way that is really easy to implement and to understand."

- CHARLES COLAW

(The co-founder of ColawFitness.com)

"We now have more money in our bank account that we've ever had."

- DAVID AND TRICIA RICH

(The founders of Pappagallos.com - Satellite Beach, Florida)

"We have grown by over 43.9% over last year."

- CHRISTINA NEMES

(Owner of Angel's Touch
www.AngelsTouchAutoDetail.com -
Bourne, Massachusetts)

Find thousands of additional testimonials today at ThrivetimeShow.com

"Genius is 1% inspiration and 99% perspiration."

- THOMAS EDISON

(The man credited with having invented the first practical light bulb, recorded audio, recorded video, and the founder of General Electric.)

```
<header>
    <p>ABOUT THE AUTHORS</p>

    <h1>
```

WHO ARE
THESE GUYS?

```
    </h1>

</header>
                        <style>
                          #page-background{
                                background-color: #0F9D58;
                          }

                            h1{
                                text-transform: uppercase;
                                color: white;
                                font-family: 'Proxima Nova';
                                font-weight: 900;
                            }
                        </style>
```

ABOUT THE AUTHORS

WHO IS CLAY CLARK?

Clay is the former U.S. SBA Entrepreneur of the Year for the state of Oklahoma, the co-host of the ThrivetimeShow.com Radio Show podcast, and the founder of ThrivetimeShow.com. Over the course of his career, he has been a founding team member of many successful companies including DJConnection.com, EITRLounge.com, MakeYourLifeEpic.com, and EpicPhotos.com (Dallas, Oklahoma City, etc.). He and his companies have been featured in Forbes, Fast Company, Entrepreneur, PandoDaily, Bloomberg TV, Bloomberg Radio, the Entrepreneur On Fire Podcast, the So Money Podcast with Farnoosh Torabi, and on countless media outlets. He's been the speaker of choice for Hewlett-Packard, Maytag University, O'Reilly Auto Parts, Valspar Paint, Farmers Insurance, and many other companies. He is the father of five kids and he is the proud owner of 40 chickens, thirteen cats, and thousands of trees. Clay is an obsessive New England Patriots fan and Tim Tebow apologist. He wears the same thing every day. When not chasing his kids and wife around, he enjoys reading business case studies and autobiographies about successful entrepreneurs while burning pinion wood. Essentially he loves learning, earning, and burning.

Welcome to the start of your success story. Discipline is the bridge between dreams and accomplishment. Remember it's hard to build a reputation based on what you intend to do. Let's go dominate and get stuff done.

Clay Clark

I'm Thom Clark's son. I miss you Dad.

My father died after a long battle with ALS in 2016.

A WORD FROM
MICHAEL LEVINE

"Clay Clark is exceptional. But more importantly, if you are thinking about attending a conference that in 2 days can really bring value to your life, I really endorse the Thrivetime Show Conference. Clay Clark and his group are exceptional people. They are deeply devoted people. My name is Michael Levine and this is totally unsolicited."

- MICHAEL LEVINE

(New York Times best-selling author and the PR consultant of choice for Nike, Prince, Michael Jackson, President Clinton, Nancy Kerrigan and 58 Academy award-winners. 38 Grammy award-winners and 43 New York Times best-selling authors - Founder of www. michaellevinemedia.com - Los Angeles, California)

A WORD FROM
CLIFTON TAULBERT

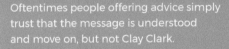

"Clay understands the hard work and dedication required and he celebrates success wherever it is found. He really does admire Napoleon Hill and fills his life with Mr. Hill's actionable quotes. They are all through this book. As I look at Clay's success and his larger-than-life vision for his future, he is well on his way to emulating the man he so admires. And quite frankly, he is placing himself in a similar position to be admired and quoted as his life and businesses continue to THRIVE.

Oftentimes people offering advice simply trust that the message is understood and move on, but not Clay Clark.

He is committed to being in your face for your success. Not afraid of repetitious conversation and in-your-face humor, he is committed to each reader getting the message and more importantly, implementing the action steps set forth in this book. Embracing and implementing the action steps in this book is the much-needed precursor to implementing the action steps around your "big idea." This man gets emotional over your business success – maximizing your talents and potential. He remembers his dorm-room start and fully celebrates yours. Quoting Clay, "My friend, as you can tell by now, running a successful business is about so much more than just having a 'big idea.' Your' big idea' is important, but the overwhelming majority of what will make your business succeed or fail has little to do with the 'big idea' itself and everything to do with the execution of the 'big idea.'" Clay leaves us no doubt that action on our part matters. His life as well as his insightful consulting encounters become a clear window through which we can look and see what is possible in many of our lives if we are willing to put in the time and effort necessary to turn ideas into reality. Clay clearly points out that our "want to" becomes the driver of our actions or lack of actions. Yes, I could have failed had I not embraced the notion that execution of a plan matters. Clay is right. His life challenges us to not settle, but to THRIVE."

CLAY CLARK &
CLIFTON TAULBERT

- CLIFTON TAULBERT

(Best-selling author, Pulitzer Prize nominee and award-winning entrepreneur whose life was turned into the Siskel and Ebert "Two Thumbs Up" movie, *Once Upon a Time When We Were Colored* starring Phylicia Rashad, Al Freedman Jr. and directed by Tim Reid)

WHO IS JONATHAN KELLY?

Jonathan Kelly is a self-made entrepreneurial success story as well as a Forbes.com contributor. He was named top 30 under 30 for Marketing and Advertising and is owner and partner of 4 different businesses. He manages a 100+ member team that helps entrepreneurs ignite their brand and increase their profit, and he also serves as the project manager for 200+ clients both nationally and internationally. Jonathan's vast knowledge of search engine optimization and advertising is unparalleled. He serves as the president of MYLEAgency.com as well as Clay Clark's business partner. He is passionate about helping entrepreneurs create, develop, and grow successful businesses. Jonathan resides in Tulsa, Oklahoma, with Stephanie, his amazing and beautiful wife, their daughter Harper Leigh, and the best bulldog on the planet, Chauncey.

"Design is not just what
it looks like and feels like,
design is how it works."

- STEVE JOBS

(Co-fonder of Apple, the
former CEO who saved PIXAR
and the founder of NeXT.)

```html
<header>

    <h1>

# INTRODUCTION

    </h1>

</header>
                    <style>
                     #page-background{
                            background-color: #4285F4;
                     }

                     h1{
                            text-transform: uppercase;
                            color: white;
                            font-family: 'Proxima Nova';
                            font-weight: 900;
                     }
                    </style>
```

Is This Book for You?

If you are a human on the planet earth, there is a good chance that you have used the internet to search for the products and services you need or want. In fact, nearly every human we have met uses their smartphone to search for the products and services that they both need and want.

THUS, WE WOULD LIKE TO ASK YOU THREE QUESTIONS:

1 How much would it be worth to you for your business to be at the top of the search results displayed by Google?

2 How much is it costing you to not be at the top of Google search engine results?

3 What terms are your ideal and likely buyers typing into the Google search bar on a daily basis to find the products and services that most closely relate to what your company offers?

If you don't know the answers to these three questions, don't freak out, that is why we wrote this book.

A Book Written for Technologically Challenged People Like Clay

The money-making internet marketing systems found within this book will help you to climb to the top of search engine results, regardless of which search engine your ideal and likely buyers are using.

If you would like to receive an audit of your website, simply take 60 seconds to fill out the form found at: ThrivetimeShow.com/Website and we will send you a detailed report for the low, low price of FREE.

You Have What It Takes.

Some people chose to not buy this book because they felt that they didn't have the "techie" background needed to make money as a result of marketing their business on the internet, but you are different. You have chosen to believe in yourself and your abilities to apply what you learn to increase what you earn. Thus, to encourage you, we have chosen to include dozens of success stories from people just like you who previously had no technical background and who are now thriving as a result of implementing the systems and processes that we have taught them over the years.

PRO TIP: ONCE YOU START GAINING MORE CUSTOMERS, MAKE SURE THAT YOU SYSTEMATICALLY **WOW** THEM!

NOTABLE QUOTABLE

"Whatever you do, do it well. Do it so well that when people see you do it, they will want to come back and see you do it again, and they will want to bring others and show them how well you do what you do."

- WALT DISNEY

(The co-founder of The Walt Disney Company who owns the record for the most Academy Awards earned by an individual)

Stop Listening to What "Most People Say." According to Forbes, 9 out of 10 Businesses Fail, Thus Most People Are Wrong:

"When you wow people they will refer you now!"
- Clay Cark

If you choose to commit yourself to doing what you've always done you are going to keep getting the same results year after year. However, if you decide to follow the proven path you will experience predictably successful results.

You Must Wow if You Want Word of Mouth Referrals Now:

Companies that wow their customers grow and companies that do not WOW their customers will not grow regardless of how much money they spend on marketing. We all know that companies like Apple, Southwest Airlines, QuikTrip, Wholefoods, Chick-fil-A, and Disney are operating at a level that is far ABOVE and BEYOND the level of their competition, which is why we love them.

However, when you break it down and try to apply this principle to your business you must ask yourself, "What is my business doing on a daily and systemic basis to WOW our customers?"

NOTABLE QUOTABLE

"A business exists to serve you."

- DOCTOR ROBERT ZOELLNER

(The founder of DrZoellner.com, Z66AA. com, DrZzzs.com, A to Z Medical, co-host of The Thrivetime Show Podcast, early stage investor in BankRegent.com, etc.)

SUCCESS STORIES

Since 2007, Clay has been hired to consult, coach and speak to hundreds of businesses including: Bama Companies, EXP Realty, Hewlett Packard, KLOrtho.com, Maytag University, OxiFresh. com, RevolutionHealth.org, TipTopK9.com, UPS, Valspar Paint, WintersKing.com, etc...

"He has always helped me with web development and search engine optimization. With his help we've been able to really keep a steady stream of clients coming in because they found us on the web. With everything that I've encountered, and everything that I experienced, I quickly learned, it is worth every penny to have someone on your team that can walk you through what works and even avoid some of the pitfalls that are almost invariable in starting your own business.

- MICKEY MICHALEC

(Capital Waste Solutions)

SUCCESS STORIES

"Being top in Google has meant the WORLD to our business. I'm so thankful for all of the work that your team has done to get us to the top. We are always the top 1, 2, or 3 in the search results for our keywords. It took us about 18-24 months and it was well worth it!"

- GUY SHEPHERD

(Founder of Shepherd Automotive - ShepherdAutomotive.com)

NOTABLE QUOTABLE

"Profit in business comes from repeat customers, customers that boast about your project or service, and that bring friends with them."

- W. EDWARDS DEMING

(A legendary author, professor and business management consultant.)

HOW MUCH IS DOMINATING THE SEARCH ENGINES WORTH TO YOU?

You have the mental capacity to learn this. Throughout the years, we've worked with and personally coached thousands of busy business owners like you and in every case, we have been able to teach anyone who was sincerely motivated to learn how to dominate search engine results. We know that search engine optimization is currently the most affordable, proven, and powerful marketing strategy available and we believe it to be a huge issue if you do not know how search engine optimization (commonly referred to as SEO) truly works. Search engine optimization should not be viewed as mysterious or overwhelming. It should be seen as just another core daily task that is executed by your business every day, just like turning the lights on and locking the doors to your business. Up to now, you probably have not learned the art of search engine optimization because...

1. You have denied that your ideal and likely buyers actually use the Internet to find both the products and services they are looking for.

2. You have read too many search engine optimization blogs and have been falsely led to believe that the Internet is too complicated and that Google is always changing radically, so even attempting to optimize your website is a waste of time.

3. You have yet to discover a system for search engine optimization that is both clear and understandable.

Why Believe Us?

If you have been in business for any number of years, you have definitely been reached out to by several "SEO firms" that were clearly scammers who promise to get you thousands of website leads each month, and "to the top of Google FAST!" If you have ever had the misfortune of responding to one of these emails or phone calls, you will quickly realize how this seems too good to be true and that is too good to be true. There are no shortcuts to ranking in Google. To rank high in Google it takes consistency, hard-work, and diligence.

We are not teaching you our personal opinions of how Google works, we are teaching you the best practice systems that have proven to work time, and time again. We have read the books, hired the top consultants, and we have distilled the system for you. We have used the system on our own companies and we've helped our clients dominate the search engine results as a result of implementing these systems as well.

To create the system that we are going to teach you in this book, please know that Clay has experimented on his own businesses first. We then successfully taught this system to hundreds of clients who have been able to create hundreds of millions of dollars of market value as a result. Clay has painstakingly invested thousands of hours into the creation of these effective search engine techniques, and has read countless best-practice search engine optimization books on the subject to create THE BEST SEARCH ENGINE OPTIMIZATION SYSTEM ON THE PLANET. If you would like to read more on the subject of search engine optimization, we highly recommend that you read the following books:

Get Rich Click
by Mark Ostrofsky – This book is endorsed by Steve Wozniak who co-founded that little company called Apple.

Search Engine Optimization for Dummies All-in-One – by Bruce Clay – This book is very detailed and has the potential to blow your mind...so be careful.

Honest Seduction: Using Post-Click Marketing to Turn Landing Pages into Game-Changers – by Scott Brinker, Anna Talerico and Justin Talerico This book teaches you how to build sincere trust and loyalty from people who have never met you in person and who have only met you online.

After you finish reading the 1,500 pages found within those 3 books about how to harness the power of internet marketing, you will be a certified nerd and we will give you a high-five when we see you in person at one of our 2-day interactive *Thrivetime Show* workshops.

However, once you know what the heck you are doing, you must then commit to being a diligent doer and not being just a happy hoper.

You must commit to actually taking the action steps that are required to win because knowledge is only potential power.

NOTABLE QUOTABLE

"I have learned from both my own successes and failures and those of many others that it's the boring stuff that matters the most. Startup success is not a consequence of good genes or being in the right place at the right time. Startup success can be engineered by following the right process, which means it can be learned, which means it can be taught."

- ERIC RIES

(Best-selling author of The Lean Startup, and a former consultant at the Kleiner Perkins Venture Capital Organization.)

Getting to the top of search engine results is not an overnight process that will immediately begin sending your business life-changing amounts of inbound leads from your website. However, we promise that if you follow these checklists that we are providing you, and if you use our proven search engine optimization rules, you will rise to page one in Google search results and you will then generate a copious amount of leads.

<strong> **LET'S DO THIS!** </strong>

STEP #1
Create a website with the proper Google compliant website architecture.

STEP #4
Gather objective Google reviews from your customers.

STEP #3
Set up and optimize your Google My Business Map / listing.

STEP #2
Create a website that is Google mobile compliant.

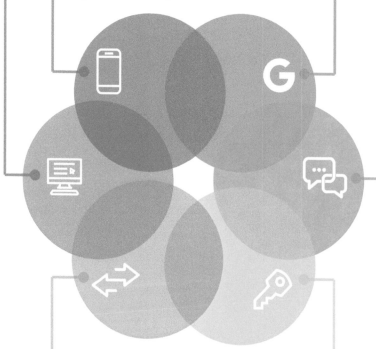

STEP #6
Generate the most high-quality backlinks possible.

STEP #5
Create the most relevant and keyword-rich original content possible.

```html
<header class="chapter-title">
    <p>CHAPTER 1</p>

    <h1>
```

SEARCH ENGINE DOMINATION

```html
    </h1>
</header>
```

```html
<style>
    #page-background{
        background-color: #F4B400;
    }
        .chapter-title p{
            text-transform: uppercase;
            color: white;
            font-family: 'Proxima Nova';
            font-weight: 600;
        }

        .chapter-title h1{
            text-transform: uppercase;
            color: white;
            font-family: 'Proxima Nova';
            font-weight: 900;
        }
</style>
```

Everyone Uses the Internet, Yet Few Know How to Market Effectively Using It.

According to research published by Pew Research in March of 2018, 77% of people now go online on a daily basis to find the answers, solutions, products, services and connections they are looking for. However, from both our personal experience and having worked with thousands of people to help them to increase their companies' value by hundreds of millions of dollars, I have personally discovered that less than 1% of the clients that we have worked with knew how search engine optimization truly worked before we taught it to them.

During the pages of this practical, action-orientated, and game-changing book, we will teach you the specific steps that you need to take in order to begin generating leads and making money as a result of learning how to dominate search engine results.

....

"Almost 90% of consumers said
they read online reviews."

- FORBES

("Online Reviews And Their Impact On The Bottom Line")

....

Search engines are used by the vast majority of people to find the products and services that they buy, yet very few people truly understand how search engines actually work.

Search engines use electronic devices commonly referred to as "spiders," "robots" (or "bots") to crawl and scan the vast internet in search of the most relevant content that they can display to search engine users.

The Most Relevant Original HTML Content + The Most Objective Reviews + The Most Mobile Compliance + The Most Google Compliance = Million$

In order to do this, search engines "index", "catalogue," and "sort" the information that is publicly available on the internet so that when a user conducts a search using a search engine they are able to find the information that is most relevant to their search terms.

In fact, here is an explanation of how Google works from Google itself, "The software behind our search technology conducts a series of simultaneous calculations requiring only a fraction of a second. Traditional search engines rely heavily on how often a word appears on a web page. We use more than 200 signals, including our patented PageRank algorithm, to examine the entire link structure of the web and determine which pages are most important. We then conduct hypertext-matching analysis to determine which pages are relevant to the specific search being conducted.

By combining overall importance and query-specific relevance, we're able to put the most relevant and reliable results first. (Corporate Information, Google).

NOTABLE QUOTABLE

"Success is a choice."

- NAPOLEON HILL

(Best-selling self-help author of all time)

Organic Search 101: 🌿

Most of the people on the planet who choose to use search engines to find the products, services, and solutions that they are looking for, are not inclined to sift through pages and pages of search engine results to find the result that they believe to be the best. In fact, most users refuse to ever even consider the search results found on page 2 of most Google search engine results. In years past, on other search engines, you could just pay to have your website ranked higher on search engine results, but Google decided to change everything and created the absolute best search engine results possible for users when they decided to not allow businesses to "pay to play" as it relates to dominating organic search engine results (although you can buy advertisements using Adwords).

Google's founders Larry Page and Sergey Brin leveled the playing field for people like us that did not grow up with silver spoons in our mouths when they decided to fill the majority of their search engine results with non-paid search engine results and content that was created by diligent people who were actually willing to invest the time needed to create Google compliant websites and content.

Design 101:

You must obsess over the concept that your website only exists to provide solutions for your ideal and likely buyers and to help you make a profit as a result of providing those solutions to your ideal and likely buyers. Many business owners spend every dime that they have on creating a visually incredible website that

"If you can't explain it simply, you don't understand it well enough."

- ALBERT EINSTEIN

(Albert Einstein was the German-born theoretical physicist that saved America. The Nazis were very close to developing nuclear bombs that they were committed to dropping on United States soil when Albert Einstein alerted our American President Franklin Delano Roosevelt of the diabolical technological advances. Only after much pleading did President FDR agree to allow America to begin investing the resources and the time needed to create our game-changing nuclear weapon at the last hour. In 1921, Einstein won the Nobel Prize in Physics.)

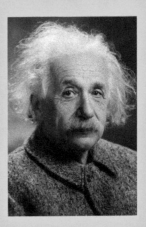

no one can ever find because it does not follow Google's search engine compliance rules.

Clay has personally employed and fired well over a dozen web-developers who refused to grasp this concept because of their fascination and preoccupation with building websites that were visually incredible and virtually undiscoverable by search engines.

The Google Domination Equation

Proper Google Website Architecture (must follow Google's canonical rules) + Proper Google Mobile Compliance + Reviews + Most Relevant Original Content + Most High Quality Backlinks = Top of Google Search Engine Results.

The bottom line is that the sites that have the most overall Google canonical compliant architecture, the most Google mobile compliant architecture, the most original relevant content and the most relevant, high quality backlinks, will win. Once you wrap your mind around this idea, you can win. However, before you can win, you must first know what search terms (also referred to as "keyword phrases") are actually winnable.

How to Determine Winnable Keywords

As an example, let's say you want your website to come up in the top of the Google search results for the search term, "San Diego Dog Training." To help you to determine if this search term is actually winnable, we will now walk you through the process.

STEP 1: Type "San Diego Dog Training" into the Google search bar and hit enter. After you skip past the Adwords, and the 2 Yelp listings, Johnknowsdogs.com currently comes came up top in the search results.

No Jonathan Kelly does not own JohnKowsDogs.com.

STEP 2: Go to SEMRush.com. SEMRush.com allows you to run a website audit on your competitor's website so you can see how they are doing (JohnKnowsDogs.com got a score of 78% and SEMRush will tell you why). It will also tell you the top keywords that JohnKnowsDogs.com is ranking for, what sites are linking to JohnKnowsDogs.com, and any ads that JohnKnowsDogs.com is running.

STEP 3: Go to https://www.google.com/webmasters/tools/mobile-friendly/ and run a report on their overall Google mobile compliance score. Unfortunately, while the page is mobile friendly, there are some issues.

STEP 4: Go to freetools.webmasterworld.com/ and click on "Indexed Pages" to determine how many pages of content the johnknowsdogs.com people have. Currently

they have 67 pages of content on their website that are
indexed in Google (Google requires each page to have
350 + words or more). Internally we require our team to
write 1,000 words on each page of the websites we write
search engine optimization content for. Another way to
check is to take their URL and simply add "Site:" in front of
the website address. *Example: Site:Eitrlounge.com*

STEP 5: Go to developers.google.com/speed/pagespeed/
insights/ to check your website speed. On mobile,
JohnKnowsDogs.com has a page speed score of 88%.

 Fun Fact: As of the time that this book was written,
Apple has an SEM Rush score of 29%. Remember, the
perfectly optimized website for Google is Wikipedia.

Equipped with this information, you now know that if you wanted to beat JohnKnowsDogs.com for the term "San Diego dog training" you would need to have the following:

» Google architecture compliance score of 78% or more.

» A Google mobile compliance score that is found to be "mobile-friendly."

» 134 pages of original content on your website (because you always want to have two times more content than your closest competition).

» A site that loads in 3 seconds or less.

» Relevant backlinks from reputable sites.

» $3,000 to fix your website to get to be both architecturally and mobile compliant.

» $26,800 to pay a search engine expert $200 per page to write 134 pages of content.

» $75 a month for a sufficient website hosting package (Godaddy Business Hosting Grow package)

Jonathan's dog, Chauncey and the average marketing professor on most college campuses will teach about the same amount when it comes to search engine domination.

Total: $29,800

*if you paid most search engine optimization firms to optimize our website for you. However, with our system it would only cost **$4,415***

DEEP THOUGHTS FROM CLAY:

Marinate on that math for a moment... For me, this number would be very encouraging both now and when I was starting my first business out of my college dorm room. I grew up without money. When I was in college, I worked at a call center, Applebee's, Target, and as an intern at Tax and Accounting Software Company. During summers I worked well over 80 hours per week as a home health aide at night and a very low-skilled concrete construction worker during the day. Without reservation, I spent over $2,000 per month on Yellow Page advertisements and nearly $1,000 per month on bridal trade show booths while I was still in college. To afford this marketing, both my wife and I decided to live without air conditioning and to operate with only one mobile phone and one car. We made sacrifices, but they paid off. If I owned a dog training company in San Diego and I just discovered that for a total of $29,800 I could beat my competition, I would be pumped and would be asking when we could get started! The excitement of this would have me salivating like a bulldog.

I am here to help you win, but I can't do that if I don't know what search terms you are trying to win. If I were you, I would not move on from this page until you've asked our team do a free audit and evaluation of your website and until you have determined your "winnable keywords." To get the ball rolling, fill out the form at ThrivetimeShow.com/ Website today.

Once you have determined your winnable keywords, it is time to begin the process of executing the proven winning strategy, which includes the following steps that we'll teach you in a minute.

JONATHAN'S GLORIOUS BULLDOG, **"CHAUNCEY"**

4 SUPER MOVES to Determine What Keywords to Optimize Your Website for:

Move 1 - Type in the search terms that YOU think your ideal and likely buyers might be searching for. As an example let's say that you think that your ideal and likely buyers might be searching for "Dallas wedding cakes." Now do a quick Google search for "Dallas wedding cakes." Don't over think this.

Move 2 - Scroll to the bottom of the search engine results and you will see "Searches related to Dallas wedding cakes." These are the keywords that YOU WANT to optimize for. But why can't it be more complicated? Because, search engine domination is not complicated, it just requires diligent consistent effort and we know that you are up to this task.

dallas wedding cakes

Coffee and dessert

Birthday cakes

Best coffee

Cake shops

Searches related to Dallas wedding cakes

cake bakery dallas	champagne cake dallas
walmart wedding cakes	frosted art bakery
custom cakes dallas	elena's cakes
panini bakery dallas	dallas cakes bakeries

Move 3 - Ask your actual customers what they would actually type into the search engines to find the products and services that you offer. Do you mean that I should actually talk to another human? Isn't there an "app" for that? Yes.

Talk to an actual human. In fact talk to hundreds of humans and ask them what keywords they would actually type into search engines to find the products and services that you offer. The vast majority of people don't all search for the same keywords. In fact well over 50% of all search engine results are not "the most popular search term."

Everybody in your town doesn't search for "business coach Denver." Some people search for "America's #1 Business Coach," some people search for "who is the best business coach?", and still others search for "business coach near me."

When searching for haircuts some people search "best mens haircuts in Tulsa" or "Jenks mens haircuts" or "haircuts in jenks" etc…

Move 4 - Go to your competition's website and then simply right click on their homepage and click "view source." There you can see the keywords that your competition is focused on optimizing for. There in their actual source code you can see their "title tags," their "meta description" and their "keyword" focus. Find what is working for them and then just out work them.

***Bonus Note - If it took you $4,415 to win a keyword, how many closed deals or in this example "dog training classes" would you need to sell in order for it to be worth it? How many sales are you missing out on by NOT being on the first page? According to Forbes, 75% of users never scroll past the first page of search results.

NOTABLE QUOTABLE

"Most people think it's all about the idea. It's not. Everyone has ideas... The hard part is to execute on the idea."

- MARK CUBAN

(The iconic entrepreneur and NBA basketball team owner of the Dallas Mavericks)

NOTABLE QUOTABLE

"Simple can be harder than complex. You have to work hard to get your thinking clean to make it simple."

- STEVE JOBS

(Co-founder of Apple, the former CEO of PIXAR, and the founder of NeXT.)

"Luck is what happens when Preparation meets opportunity." - Seneca

(Famous roman stoic philosopher, dramatist, and statesman)

SUCCESS STORIES 🏆

"We began with very few leads. So what's happening? We've doubled our incoming leads."

- CHRIS DE JESUS

(Owner of Breakout Creative)
- See their success at
BreakoutCreativeCompany.)

SUCCESS STORIES 🏆

"When we started, if you put my name in exactly spelled correctly, you might've found me on 20 pages back. So, we started from scratch and now we're climbing the Google search engine each day. That's a nice, new thing. People come in and are like, "Hey, I saw you online. Literally, from a year and a half ago to now, we're up double."

- DR. BRECK KASBAUM

(Founder of Dr. Breck
Kasbaum Chiropractor
- See his success at
www.DrBreck.com)

SUCCESS STORIES 🏆

"Clay taught me how to put a website together, how to optimize the website, how to blog, and how to use social media because we had an old school website and I think we got maybe 50 website visits a month. And then once we improved our website as part of the business coaching for bridal shops program from Clay, we started getting more calls and more calls. And I mean, I think our highest number so far has been up in 3,000s and we get more people walking in. Obviously the more customers that we can speak with, the more people we can sell our product to. I believe that the training that you get here is going to be the best money spent."

- JENNIFER THOMPSON

(Founder of Facchianos Bridal
- See her success at Facchianos.com)

NOTABLE QUOTABLE

"I have been impressed with the urgency of doing. Knowing is not enough; we must apply. Being willing is not enough; we must do. "

- LEONARDO DA VINCI

(An epic polymath who taught himsef to be a master at invention, drawing, painting, sculpting, and more.)

CHAPTER 2

ULTIMATE SEARCH ENGINE DOMINATION CHECKLIST

In order for you to achieve total SEARCH ENGINE DOMINATION and DRAMATICALLY increase your level of COMPENSATION you must simply check off and complete all of the checklist items on this website evaluation. We humbly refer to this checklist as "The Ultimate Search Engine Domination Checklist."

The Ultimate Search Engine DOMINATION Checklist
(and Website Evaluation):

_____ **Host your website with a reliable hosting service**. If your website is hosted with an unreliable hosting service you will rank lower in the search engines. We recommend using GoDaddy.com. Don't host your website with some local, janky hosting provider who lives with his mom in the basement.

_____ **Host your website with the fastest package that you can afford.** Google REALLY CARES about how long it takes for your website to load. Why? Because people get impatient and will quickly move on to another website if your website takes too long to load. On January 17th of 2018, Google formally announced the "Speed Update." Google's plan called for them to slowly roll out the new search engine ranking criteria to give web-developers plenty of time to make their websites load much, much faster. To test the speed of your website visit: https://developers.google.com/speed/pagespeed/insights/ To read more about Google's new speed requirements visit: https://www.forbes.com/sites/jaysondemers/2018/01/29/will-googles-new-page-speed-criteria-affect-your-site/#396634ed6a8f

_____ **Build your website on the WordPress platform**. "WordPress offers the best out-of-the-box search engine optimization imaginable." - Tim Ferriss (Best-selling author of *The 4-Hour Work Week*, *The 4-Hour Body*, *The 4-Hour Chef*, *Tools of Titans*, and *Tribe of Mentors*. He is also an early stage investor in Facebook, Twitter, Evernote, Uber, etc.)

Don't use any other website building platform than WordPress. If you hire coders to custom build your website on PHP or .NET you will end up hating your life as a result of having a website that nobody can update other than the entitled, nefarious employees who now have the ability to hold you hostage. Trust us here. We have personally coached hundreds of clients and every time our coaching clients have a custom built website the business owner at some point has been held hostage by the employee who is the only person who knows how to update the custom built, non-search engine friendly, and ridiculously complicated website. Building your website on WordPress puts the power back in your hands as a business owner because you can update the website yourself if you have to.

PRO TIP: USE WORDPRESS.ORG NOT WORDPRESS.COM

WordPress.org is the open source platform used to power the best SEO compliant websites in the world. WordPress.com is their platform that does not allow for plugins or optimal website optimization.

*Avoid WordPress.com

_____ **Build a mobile-friendly website.** What is a mobile friendly website? Check your website's mobile compliance at: https://search.google.com/test/mobile-friendly. If this link changes in the future just search for "Google mobile compliance test" in the Google search engine and you'll find it.

_____ Install HTTPS encryption onto your website.
HTTPS encryption stands for Hypertext Transfer Protocol Secure. What does that mean? HTTPS encryption makes your website more difficult for bad people to hack, thus making it tougher for very bad people to crash your website and to use your website as a way to steal the personal information of your valuable clients and patrons. Google ranks websites higher who have invested the additional money needed to add HTTPS encryption to their website. How many times would you use Google if every time their search results sent you to websites that had been hacked into by cyber criminals and internet hackers?

_____Install the Yoast.com search engine optimization plugin into your website. What is Yoast? Yoast SEO is the best WordPress plugin on the planet when it comes to search engine optimization. Yoast was built and designed in a way to make search engine optimization approachable for everyone, and thus we love Yoast. Yoast makes it possible for people who are not complete nerds to proactively manage the search engine optimization of their website.

DEFINITION MAGICIAN
Plugin - A plugin is a piece of code or software that provides a variety of functions that you can add to your WordPress website. Plugins allow you to increase the functional capacity of your website without having to hire a bunch of nefarious, entitled custom coders who are typically hard to manage because you do not have any idea what they are working on or what they are talking about 90% of the time.

_____Uniquely optimize every meta title tag on every page of your website.
The title tag is simply a hypertext markup language (HTML) element on a website that specifies to search engines what a particular web page is all about. "according to SEOMoz, the best practice for the title tag length is to keep titles under 70 characters." An example would be, "Full Package Media I Dallas Real Estate Photography I 972-885-8823"

Full Package Media | Dallas Real Estate Photography | 972-885-8823
https://fullpackagemedia.com/ ▾
Looking for the best in the business when it comes to **Dallas** Real Estate Photography? You need to

_____Uniquely optimize every meta description on every page of your website. The meta description is simply part of the hypertext markup language (HTML) code that provides a brief summary about a web page. Search engines like Google usually show the meta description in search engine results. Don't make your meta descriptions more than 160 characters in length.

An ample example would be, "Looking for the best in the business when it comes to Dallas Real Estate Photography? You need to call Full Package Media today at 972-885-8823."

Looking for the best in the business when it comes to **Dallas** Real Estate Photography? You need to call **Full Package Media** today at 972-885-8823.
Careers · About Us · Contact Us · Client Login

_____Uniquely optimize the keywords on every page of your website. Meta keywords are a very specific kind of meta tag that will show up in the hypertext markup language (HTML) code on web pages and these will tell the search engines what the web page is really all about. An example of specific keyword optimization would be "Berj Najarian." You may be thinking, who is Berj Najarian?

Berj Najarian serves as the New England Patriots Director of Football and the "Chief of Staff" for the legendary Coach Bill Belichick who has won a total of 8 Super Bowl titles since beginning his coaching career in the National Football League. If someone is searching for "Berj Najarian" there is a high probability that they already know who "Berj Najarian" is and if you want to rank high in the search engines when people are searching for "Berj Najarian" you definitely want to make sure that you have declared your meta keyword phrase as "Berj Najarian."

Quick Note: If at any point while reading this you are beginning to feel overwhelmed just submit your website for an audit and deep dive evaluation and we'll do the heavy lifting for you. You can submit your website to be audited at: www.ThrivetimeShow.com/Website

 _____ **Create 1,000 words of original and relevant text (content) per page on your website.** Are we saying that somebody actually has to write, 1,000 original words of original and relevant text for every page of your website? Yes. Isn't there a hack? NO. Can't there be a better way? No.

Can't you just go out and hire a company out of India to use "spinners" to slightly change existing text for you? NO. Can't you just copy content from another website? NO.

You can spend every minute of every day trying to find some blogger or some website experts out there that will tell you that someone on your team doesn't need to invest the time needed to create 1,000 words of both original and relevant content and you will eventually find them and they will be 100% wrong. However, they will gladly take your money.

Google   berj najarian

All   Images   News   Shopping   Videos   More   Settings   Tools

About 6,450 results (0.38 seconds)

META TITLE TAG

Who is Berj Najarian? | Bill Belichick's Secret Weapon | Thrivetimeshow
https://www.thrivetimeshow.com/.../berj-najarian-the-80-20-rule-the-new-england-pat... ▾
★★★★★ Rating: 4.9 · 2,651 reviews
Berj Najarian is Bill Belichick's Chief of Staff he's the human on the planet that has spent the most time with Bill Belichick since he became the New England ...

PERMALINK

META DESCRIPTION

Who is the mysterious Berj Najarian, Bill Belichick's right-hand man ...
https://www.bostonglobe.com/sports/patriots/2019/01/31/...berj-najarian.../story.html
Jan 31, 2019 · Najarian is one of the most powerful figures on the Boston sports landscape, yet most fans have never heard of him.

Images for berj najarian

→   More images for berj najarian   Report images

YOU OR A MEMBER OF YOUR TEAM MUST WRITE
1,000 WORDS OF ORIGINAL AND RELEVANT
CONTENT FOR EVERY PAGE OF YOUR WEBSITE.

_____ **Create a Google search engine compliant
.XML sitemap on your website.** What is an .XML
sitemap? XML stands for Extensible Markup Language.
A quality XML sitemap serves as a map of your website
which allows the Google search engine to find all of
the important pages located within your website. As a
website owner unless you hate money, you REALLY WANT
GOOGLE to be able to crawl (find, rank, and sort) all
of the important pages on your website. Yoast.com has
tools that will actually generate Google compliant .XML
sitemaps for you. Don't worry, you can do this!

😊 ***Fun Fact:*** *I had to take Algebra 3 times en route
to getting into Oral Roberts University and I
was eventually kicked out of college for writing
a parody about the school's president "ORU
Slim Shady" which you can currently find on
YouTube. If I can learn and master search engine
optimization you can too!*

_____Create a Google search engine compliant HTML sitemap. What's an HTML site map? A hypertext markup language sitemap allows the people who visit your website to easily navigate your website. This sitemap should be located at the bottom of your website and should be labeled as a "Sitemap."

Hiding your sitemap for any reason is a bad idea because Google assumes that if you are hiding your sitemap you are probably trying to hide something. Don't change the background of your website to be the same color as your sitemap's font or do anything tricky here. You want to make sure that your website's sitemap can easily be found at the bottom of your website. See the example below:

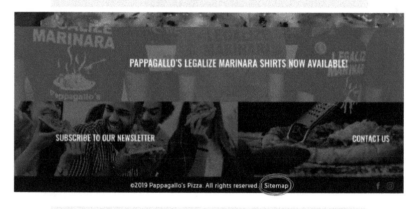

_____Create a clickable phone number. If you ever want to sell something to humans on the planet Earth you must make your contact information easy to find. Thus you want to make your phone number easily available to find at either the top right or at the bottom of your website. When coaching your web-developer, force them to make your phone number a "click-to-call" phone number so that users on your website who are using a mobile phone (almost everyone) can simply click the number to call you.

In our shameless attempt to make this the BEST, MOST
HUMBLE and the MOST ACTIONABLE SEARCH
ENGINE OPTIMIZATION book of all time we have
provided the following real examples from REAL
clients just like you who we have really helped to
REALLY increase their REAL sales year after year:

_____**Have a Social Proof.** If you don't hate money and you are not a committed socialist, you will want to include some social proof near the top of your website. What is social proof? "Social proof" is a phrase and a term that was original created by the best-selling author Robert Cialdini in his book, *Influence*. The best social proof examples are:

a. Real testimonials from real current and former clients is super powerful.

b. Media features and appearances on credible media sources like Bloomberg, Fox Business, Entrepreneur.com, Fast Company, etc.

c. Proudly showing that you have earned the highest and most reviews in your local business niche.

d. Celebrity endorsements from celebrities that have earned the trust of your ideal and likely buyers.

e. Listed below is an example that will showcase to you what it looks like to use social proof effectively.

_____Make the logo return to home. Allow the logo on your website to serve as your "homepage" button. As of 2019, most people assume that if they click your logo they are going to be taken back to the homepage of your website.

 _____Create original content. You must create more original and relevant content than anyone else in the world about your specific search engine focus. If you want to come up top in the world for the phrase "organic supplements" you must then create the most original and relevant content on the planet about "organic supplements." If you want to come up top in your city for the phrase "knee pain Tulsa" then you must what? You must create the most original and relevant content on the planet about "knee pain Tulsa."

If you want to come up top in the search engine results for the phrase "America's #1 business coach" then you must create the most original and relevant content on the planet about "America's #1 business coach." Listed below are a few examples of receiving high search rankings due to having the most original, relevant content on the planet about that particular subject.

---

america's #1 business coach 　　　　　　　　　🎤　🔍

All　News　Images　Videos　Maps　More　　　Settings　Tools

About 5,870,000 results (0.35 seconds)

Business Coach | Bill Belichick's #1 Fan and America's #1 Business ...
https://www.thrivetimeshow.com/the...show/business-coach-management-principles/ ▼
★★★★★ Rating: 99% - 2,651 votes
Bill Belichick's number one fan and **America's #1 business coach** Clay Clark teaches many of the successful management principles that Belichick ...

People also ask

Who is the best business coach in the world?　　　　　　　⌄

What should I look for in a business coach?　　　　　　　⌄

1.3 mi · 3019 E 101st St · (918) 299-4415 ext. 5384   WEBSITE   DIRECTIONS

The Little Gym of SE Tulsa
4.7 ★★★★★ (14) · Gymnastics center
3.3 mi · 6556 E 91st St · (918) 492-2626
Open · Closes 7:30PM   WEBSITE   DIRECTIONS
🌐 Their website mentions **gymnastics classes**

Twist & Shout Tumbling & Cheer
3.5 ★★★★☆ (8) · Gym
6.2 mi · 4820 S 83rd E Ave · (918) 622-5857
Closed · Opens 5PM   WEBSITE   DIRECTIONS
🌐 Their website mentions **tumbling classes**

☰ More places

Tumbling Tulsa | Tulsa Tumbling Lessons | 918-764-8804
https://justicetumblingco.com/ ▾
If you are looking for the best and highest reviewed **tumbling Tulsa** place, you need to call us at Justice
Tumbling today and see what makes us better.
Services · About · Schedule · Testimonials

Tulsa Cheerleading | Tumbling Tulsa | Tulsa Tumbling | 918-986-5785
https://tumblesmart.com/ ▾
Tulsa's Most Reviewed **Tumbling** Program. **Tumble** Smart Athletics. Free Evaluation **Lesson**Meet the
Owner. **Tumbling Tulsa** Gymnast Stars. Experience the

Google   tulsa knee pain   🎤   🔍

META TITLE TAG

Tulsa Knee Pain - Revolution Health Tulsa
https://www.revolutionhealth.org/.../tulsa-knee-pain-revolution-health-is-bring-in-a-re... ▾
Find the best treatment for your **Tulsa knee pain** right here in Tulsa. Find out more about Revolution
Health by calling at 918-935-3636.   *META DESCRIPTION*

PERMALINK

Tulsa knee Pain | Revolution Health Oklahoma
https://www.revolutionhealth.org/.../tulsa-knee-pain-find-the-top-and-quickest-result-f... ▾
The best prolotherapy is right here at Revolution Health for **Tulsa knee pain.**

Best Prolotherapy Treatments Tulsa | Tulsa Knee Pain
https://www.revolutionhealth.org/.../tulsa-knee-pain-find-the-best-possible-tulsa-knee-... ▾
Best Prolotherapy Treatments for your **tulsa knee Pain**

Non-invasive remedies relieve knee pain without surgery - Tulsa World
https://www.tulsaworld.com/...knee-pain.../article_6bdf681d-d017-554c-9ecc-fae529... ▾
Mar 13, 2019 · Dear Doctor K: I have osteoarthritis of the knee. Are there ways to relieve my **knee pain**
without drugs or surgery?

_____**Create a "Testimonials," "Case Studies," or a "Success Stories" portion of your website** if you want to sell something to humans who were not born yesterday. Most shoppers today have become savvy and are aware of the fact that great companies generate great reviews (and occasionally bad ones) and that bad companies chronically generate bad reviews (and occasionally some good ones). Thus, most people will want to actually see testimonials, case studies or success stories from real clients that have actually worked with your company in the past.

In fact, not having testimonials, case studies, and success stories on your website freaks most people out to the point that they won't even call you or fill out your contact form.

How do we know this? Well, for starters, we are humans who happen to be also consumers and Forbes tells us that, "Almost 90% of consumers said they read reviews for local businesses. In other words, if you are not investing efforts into online reputation management, then you are missing out on having control of the first impression your business has." - *Online Reviews and Their Impact On the Bottom* Line by Matt Bowman - https://www.forbes.com/sites/forbesagencycouncil/2019/01/15/online-reviews-and-their-impact-on-the-bottom-line/#35d3b4955bde

NOTABLE QUOTABLE

"Perfectionism is often an excuse for procrastination."

- PAUL GRAHAM

(The entrepreneur investor, incubator, and coach behind AirBNB, Dropbox, and Reddit)

_____**Include a compelling 60-second video / commercial (on the top portion above the fold) on your website** to improve your conversion rate. To provide you with an ample example of clients that we have personally worked with who have used a "website header video" in route to dramatically increasing their sales check out:

VIDEO PLAY BUTTON

_____ **Create a "top of the website" call to action** that your ideal and likely buyers will relate to and connect with. You want to make it SUPER EASY for your ideal and likely buyers to call you, to schedule an appointment with you, or for them to do business with you in the most convenient way possible. As an AMPLE EXAMPLE check out EITRLounge.com and OXIFresh.com:

_____ **Create a "No-Brainer" sales offer deal** that is so GOOD, so HOT, and so IRRESISTIBLE that your ideal and likely buyers simply cannot resist the urge to at least try out your services and products out. As an example, we would encourage you to check out the following websites.

NOTABLE QUOTABLE

"Genius is 1% inspiration and 99% perspiration."

- THOMAS EDISON

(The inventor of the first practical light bulb, recorded audio, recorded video, and the founder of General Electric)

SUCCESS STORIES 🏆

"Being top in Google has impacted our business tremendously. Knowing that we're top in Google makes it so much easier for our clients to search and if they use certain keywords that pertain to our business, we're the first ones that come up on that page. We get a lot of phone call and website traffic. I would suggest every one takes this program seriously."

- MYRON KIRKPATRICK

(Founder of White Glove Auto - WhiteGloveAutoTulsa.com)

Saying, "I'm not good with computers" is not a viable strategy. I've taught this system to people in their 20's, 30's, 40's, 50's and 60's, and the coachable people have all been willing to both learn and apply it.

Before you throw up your hands and say "I'm just not tech savvy" you must understand that I do not have a college degree and yet I have been able to produce millions of dollars of revenue as a result of diligently implementing the systems that we are about to teach you. I took Algebra 3 times to graduate from high school and I had to take my ACT 3 times to be allowed into the college of my choice (Oral Roberts University) and yet I have been able to produce millions of dollars of revenue for myself and hundreds of millions of dollars of revenue for both myself and my clients. If you are willing to put in the work, the systems that I am going to teach you throughout this book will change your life."

- CLAY CLARK

(Member of the Forbes Coaching Council who's been featured in Bloomberg, Fast Company, Entrepreneur, etc.)

```html
<header class="chapter-title">
        <p>CHAPTER 3</p>
        <h1>
```

SEARCH ENGINE 101: HOW DOES GOOGLE WORK

```html
        </h1>
</header>
                <style>
                    #page-background{
                        background-color: #0F9D58;
                    }
                        .chapter-title p{
                            text-transform: uppercase;
                            color: white;
                            font-family: 'Proxima Nova ';
                            font-weight: 600;
                        }

                        .chapter-title h1{
                            text-transform: uppercase;
                            color: white;
                            font-family: 'Proxima Nova';
                            font-weight: 900;
                        }
                    }
                </style>
```

SUCCESS STORIES 🏆

"It's been great just being able to know where everything is going and where it's coming from has been a huge relief, stress off my shoulders. Just being able to look at a spreadsheet and say oh yeah, we made $800 off of $50 invested in Google. Where before I would run advertising on the radio and not even be able to tell you how much I made off of it."

- KELLY HERNISON

(Founder of American Document Shredding - See his success at WeShredOnSite.com)

How does Google work

Search engine optimization is about getting in front of your ideal and likely buyers who are currently searching for the solutions your company provides. If you are not on page one of Google's search engine results, you are invisible to customers...which is only cool if you are trying to hide from additional revenue, customers, and money.

Who Is Truly in Charge of Google Search Engine Results?

Google earns money by creating the best search engine results possible for people who search the Internet. If no one was using Google's search engine because the results that they are displaying are not logical and relevant,

"My name is Roy Coggshall. I'm from Tulsa, Oklahoma. I also have a place in Marina Del Rey, California. Actually, I am a client of Clay Clark and he's helped me move the numbers on two of my businesses. One of my friends was his client and he helped his marketing go up 1200% in three months, so that's how I got hooked up with Clay Clark. I've got two automotive businesses and I'm a technician by trade, so this is a whole new field for me. I'm really enjoying learning about people and about marketing, systems, and processes."

- Roy Coggeshall
(Owner of RC Auto Specialists and Roy's Garage) - See his success at RCAutoSpecialists.com and TheGarageBA.com

soon Google would not be able to make any money from selling advertising. Thus, Google is obsessed with making sure that their search engine results are the best in the world. As it relates to search engines, Google is the boss, the referee, the judge, and always the final word on what website is deemed to be the "most relevant" website. If you follow their rules, you will win. If you choose to not follow their rules for artistic, personal, psychological, religious, political, or emotional reasons, you will lose.

When in doubt, refer to Wikipedia. Google loves Wikipedia in the way that Clay will always love Coach Bill Belichick and the New England Patriots National Football League team. Google loves Wikipedia because Wikipedia has chosen to follow all of their rules of search engine optimization on a mass scale. Now, the W3C helps maintain and improve standards of the internet.

 FUN FACT: The World Wide Web Consortium (W3C) is made up of member organizations which maintain full-time staff for the purpose of working together in the development of standards for the World Wide Web.

You Are Never Done Tending to Your Search Engine Garden:

Search engines are always looking for the most relevant and up-to-date search engine friendly content. Thus, in order to come up top in organic search engine results you must commit your organization (and yourself) to becoming the true expert and authority of your industry/niche. You must constantly produce fresh content on a monthly, weekly or daily basis if your want to TRULY DOMINATE SEARCH ENGINE RESULTS.

The Google Story: The Timeline of the Company that Changed the Way We Use the Internet:

The two men who dropped out of college to create one of the world's most valuable companies: Larry page and Sergey Brin.

1995 - Larry Page and Sergey Brin met each other on the campus of Stanford University.

1996 - While studying to earn their PhDs from Stanford, Larry and Sergey begin working together to create a way to organize the internet they were calling BackRub, which was, named after the search engine's ability to determine what websites are the most relevant based upon the number of total backlinks a website had. In August of 1996, the very first edition of Google was shared with the world and was hosted on Stanford's website at: Google.Stanford.Edu.

1997 - Google.com was registered as the actual domain.

1998 - As an unincorporated company (thus not a company), Larry Page and Sergey Brin received their first investment of $100,000 from the co-founder of Sun Microsystems, Andy Bechtolsheim. With their early seed capital, Larry and Sergey decided to drop out of college (as most great founders do) and to setup a workspace in the garage of Susan Wojcicki (now the CEO of YouTube) in Silicon Valley. On September 7th of 1998, Larry and Sergey filed to incorporate the company. September 7th is now the date referred to as Google's birth date.

1999 - After 2 years of working for free, Larry and Sergey outgrew their garage office and they decided to move into an office with 8 employees. At this point after relentlessly pursuing investment capital, Larry and Sergey received a $25 million round of equity funding led by the good folks at the legendary venture capital funds, Sequoia Capital and Kleiner Perkins Caufield & Byers.

2000 - Larry and Sergey focused on releasing the first 10 language versions of Google including; Finnish, Norwegian, Swedish, Dutch, Spanish, French, German, Italian, Portuguese, and Danish. During this same year they secured a deal with Yahoo! to

NOTABLE QUOTABLE

"There is a creeping tendency to use made up acronyms at SpaceX. Excessive use of made up acronyms is a significant impediment to communication and keeping communication good as we grow is incredibly important. Individually, a few acronyms here and there may not seem so bad, but if a thousand people are making these up, over time the result will be a huge glossary that we have to issue to new employees. No one can actually remember all these acronyms and people don't want to seem dumb in a meeting, so they just sit there in ignorance. This is particularly tough on new employees. That needs to stop immediately or I will take drastic action - I have given enough warning over the years. Unless an acronym is approved by me, it should not enter the SpaceX glossary."

- ELON MUSK

(The man and the mind behind Tesla, SpaceX, PayPal, NeuraLink.com, Solarcity, etc.)

become its default search provider. Basically, "back-in-the-day" when you were searching using Yahoo! You were actually using Google's search engine algorithm. During this same year, Google also became the largest search engine on the planet as they proudly became the first search engine to index (organize, sort, and rank) one billion URLs (websites).

DEFINITION MAGICIAN

URL - When you hear the term URL, what you should be hearing is a "uniform resource locator (URL)." Basically, this is the address of a resource (website) that can be found on the internet.

2001 - Google decides to buy Deja.com's Usenet Discussion Service, an archive of 500 million discussions dating back to 1995. During this same year, Eric Schmidt is chosen to become the company's chairman and chief executive officer.

....

"Genius is one percent inspiration and ninety-nine percent perspiration."

- THOMAS EDISON

(The legendary inventor of recorded sound, recorded video, the first practical lightbulb, and the founder of GE)

....

NOTABLE QUOTABLE

"The fastest way to change yourself is to hang out with people who are already the way you want to be."

- REID HOFFMAN
(The co-founder of LinkedIn and a partner at the venture capital fund, Greylock Partners)

Larry Page and Sergey Brin then chose to become president(s) of the company's products and technology.

2002 - Google announced a major partnership with AOL and Google news was launched, starting with 4,000 sources.

2003 - This year was an exciting year for Google for many reasons, but at this time more and more people began to refer to "Googling" something as a "verb." In fact, the American Dialect Society members voted and decided that "Google" was most useful word of the year for 2002. During this same year, the Eric Schmidt lead Google decided to acquire Pyra Labs (the people behind the creation of Blogger).

2004 - This was another game-changing year for Google and a year in which the company launched the most popular email service on the planet called Gmail. During this same year, Eric Schmidt, Larry Page and Sergey Brin decided to take the company public with an initial public offering value of $85 per share. During this epic year of game-changing growth, Google also announced that it had partnered with leading universities to digitally scan millions of books from their collections.

2005 - Google launched the technology that has now morphed into the world's most popular global positioning system and turn-by-turn navigation application (Google Maps and Google Earth). This technology is powered by a satellite imagery-based mapping service. At this time Larry and Sergey were both 30 years old. As more and more users began using Google, the

Washington Post reported that Google posted a 700% increase in their third quarter profits alone because massive companies were shifting their advertising dollars from newspapers, television, magazines, TV and billboards to Google advertising.

2006 - At this time, Larry and Sergey were both 31 years old and they decided to acquire YouTube.com from Chad Hurley and Jawed Karim for $1.65 billion. In October 2006, Larry and Sergey moved forward with their decision to purchase the second largest search engine in the world, YouTube.com. This epic deal was completed on November 13, 2006.

 FUN FACT – YouTube TV is now growing virally and is on the verge of replacing cable and satellite TV all together.

2006 - Google experienced dramatic growth when they decided to launch their services in China (which had a population of well over 1 billion versus the United States which had a total population of just over 300 million people).

 FUN FACT – The verb "google" was officially added to the English language as a verb in 2006. It was added to the Oxford English Dictionary on June 15, 2006, and to the eleventh edition of the Merriam-Webster Collegiate Dictionary in July 2006.

2007 – Larry and Sergey were both 32 years old. **The $3 billion dollar purchase very few people talk about:** On April 13th of 2007, Google was able to reach a deal to acquire DoubleClick for $3.1 billion. DoubleClick worked with major websites to serve the digital advertisements of massive companies to website visitors.

"Basically, our goal is to organize the world's information and to make it universally accessible and useful."

- Larry Page
(Co-founder of Google)

Some of the accounts managed by DoubleClick included: Apple, Nike, Coca-Cola, L'Oréal, Microsoft and General Motors.

2008 – Larry and Sergey were both 33 years old – Google worked with a company called GeoEye to send a satellite to space to provide Google with high-resolution images of the planet Earth. The satellite itself was launched from the Vandenberg Air Force Base in Lompoc, California on September 6, 2008.

2011 – Larry and Sergey were both 36 years old – 15 Years into business, they made their largest ever acquisition.

On August 15, 2011, Google decided to make its biggest purchase ever when it bought Motorola Mobility for $12.5 billion. Larry Page said the move was made to increase Google's patent portfolio. Since that time Google has also began producing smartphones designed to beat Apple's iPhone in the marketplace.

2012 – 16 Years after its funding, Google hits $50 billion of annual revenue.

The year 2012 was the first time that Google generated $50 billion in annual revenue, which dramatically surpassed the $38 billion that was generated the previous year. In January 2013, then-CEO Larry Page commented, "We ended 2012 with a strong quarter ... Revenues were up 36% year-on-year, and 8% quarter-on-quarter. And we hit $50 billion in revenues for the first time last year – not a bad achievement in just a decade and a half."

> "We had our highest grossing month ever. We started from scratch and we now have 267 reviews and we're climbing the Google search engine every day. Now we are up double over last year."
> **- Dr. Breck Kasbaum**
> - See his success at drbreck.com

2014 – Larry and Sergey are both 37 years old – 18 years into their existence, the shotgun is now their approach to product creation because Google is flush with cash and is producing both consistent and massive profits. The company is focused on dramatically changing the world with substantial investments into: Self-driving cars, global positioning systems, YouTubeTV, artificial intelligence, smartphone development, search engine optimization, email, etc.

NOTABLE QUOTABLE

"The size and scope of Google's dominance now officially scares and impresses me."

- CLAY CLARK

(Founder of the *Thrivetime Show* podcast and Radio show)

Why Is Google Always Changing?

Google is focused on providing the most relevant search engine results possible so they can convince most people, like us to use their search engine when we are looking for the products, services and answers that we both want and need. The more people that are using Google, the more money they can charge advertisers to reach the people who are using Google. As technology has evolved, Google has had to evolve as well. As Google evolves, your business must also evolve if you want your customers to continue to be able to find you when they are searching on the Internet.

The Magic Begins on Mobile

We must design our websites to look great on mobile devices because this is what the majority of Internet users are using to view our websites. We also must also design our websites to look and work great on mobile devices because Google now requires websites to meet its mobile compliance standards if they are going to rank highly in search engine results. To see how high or low Google is ranking your mobile website, fill out the form at ThrivetimeShow.com/Website.

NOTABLE QUOTABLE

"A pessimist sees the difficulty in every opportunity; an optimist sees the opportunity in every difficulty."

- WINSTON CHURCHILL

(The former prime minister who famously stood up to Adolf Hitler during World War II)

To make sure you fully understand the necessary components of our search engine optimization system, we will first cover how our system works, then we will teach you how to do it. In order to dominate in the Google search engine results, you must take the following action steps laid out in the next chapters.

SIDE TIP FOR SEO SUCCESS

"IN THE WORLD OF ENTREPRENEURSHIP, PHD STANDS FOR "PIG-HEADED DISCIPLINE," BECAUSE WITHOUT IT, YOU WILL LOSE."

CLAY CLARK
(Google Certified Specialist)

NOTABLE QUOTABLE

"You should set goals beyond your reach so you can always have something to live for."

- TED TURNER

(The founder of CNN, TBS, and Turner Enterprises which manages over 51,000 bison across the various Turner properties and ranches.)

 Fun Fact: Google's Chief Executive Officer, Sundar Pichai has said that Google is focused on "A.I." first and not "Mobile first."

SUCCESS STORIES 🏆

"The number of customers we've had is up 411% over last year. We are on the top of Google. We went from non-existent to the top of page 1 by following the system."

- JARED & JENNIFER JOHNSON

(Platinum Pest & Lawn - See their success at Platinum-PestControl.com)

SUCCESS STORIES 🏆

"It took us about 5-6 months to get to the top in Google's search results, and the process has been phenomenal. Night and Day difference with the amount of business coming in between calls coming in, walk-ins, and referrals, it has been through-the-roof! We're up 50% from the previous year."

- CHRISTINA NEMES

(Owner of Angel's Touch
Auto Reconditioning
AngelsTouchAutoDetail.com)

```html
<header class="chapter-title">
    <p>
```

CHAPTER 4

```html
    <h1>
```

CREATE A WEBSITE WITH THE PROPER GOOGLE COMPLIANT WEBSITE ARCHITECTURE

```html
    </h1>

</header>
<style>
    #page-background{
        background-color: #4285F4;
    }

        .chapter-title p{
            text-transform: uppercase;
            color: white;
            font-family: 'Proxima Nova';
            font-weight: 600;
        }

        .chapter-title h1{
            text-transform: uppercase;
            color: white;
            font-family: 'Proxima Nova';
            font-weight: 900;
        }
    </style>
```

Create a website with the proper Google compliant website architecture.

Your website must follow Google's canonical rules if you want it to rank highly in the search engine results. Your website must follow the Google compliance checklist, which is available at www.ThrivetimeShow.com/Website. If you are a normal human, you are probably totally unaware of how your website ranks in terms of its overall architecture and canonical compliance. Don't let this overwhelm you. Fill out the form located at Thrivetimeshow.com/Website and we will walk you through the entire process to meet these standards. There are many different aspects that you must master to create a website that is Google compliant.

THESE INCLUDE THINGS SUCH AS:

- » **Speed of the website**
- » **Hosting with a consistent provider**
- » **Page optimization**
- » **Image optimization**
- » **HTML sitemap optimization**

- » **Strategic meta titles**
- » **Strategic meta descriptions**
- » **HTTPS encryption**
- » **Relevant original content**
- » **XML sitemap**

Bonus Note:

A website domain, is often just called a domain. Most often a website domain is created to be a memorable name to stand in the place of the numeric and almost impossible to remember IP address of a website. By choosing a domain name that is memorable, you are creating a way for visitors to both find and return to your website more easily. As a little FUN FACT and example: The domain CarInsurance.com, was sold for $49.7 million, VacationRentals.com was sold was $35 million and Hotels.com was actually sold for $11 million. Thus, we should always focus on choosing domains that our ideal and likely buyers can find easily.

NOTABLE QUOTABLE

"A good plan violently executed now is better than a perfect plan next week."

- GENERAL GEORGE PATTON

(The famous United States Army General who commanded the U.S. seventh army in the Mediterranean theatre of World War II and the U.S. Third Army in France and Germany following the allied invasion of Normandy in June of 1944.)

If you are already feeling overwhelmed, do not fear... we will break down each step during the pages of this book.

What Things Do I Need to Create a Website?

Definition - A **domain** is the web address that users would type into their web browser to go directly to your website.

1.   **A Domain** - We recommend purchasing your domain through GoDaddy.com.

2.   **Hosting** - What is Hosting? Web hosting is where your actual website files are stored. Hosting is essentially a house. Your domain or URL is the address to tell people how to find that house. You can purchase hosting through several different companies, but we recommend GoDaddy because of their 24/7 support, competitive pricing, and reliable quality. We recommend the GoDaddy Grow Package which you can purchase and save money by going to ThrivetimeShow.com/Godaddy

3.   **Content Management System (Commonly referred to as CMS)** - We recommend using WordPress.org to build your website. (this allows you to have a website without having to know how to code HTML, CSS, and PHP. This is the easiest out-of-the-box solution for Google compliance).

 Fun Fact: WordPress was developed by Matt Mullenweg and Mike Little in January, 2003.

How to Improve the Website Speed

Google puts a huge emphasis on the speed of your website when it comes to search engine rankings and it is pretty straightforward as to why. How many seconds are you willing to wait on a website to load before getting frustrated and going to a new site or giving up? This is a much different world than the dial-up ages where if you could get on a website in under 5 minutes you were happy. It is a different world now and Google will not rank websites that are not loading very quickly. Try to keep your website load time between 2-5 seconds max.

Several things you can do in order to speed up your website:

Use Cloudflare.com to create a caching/CDN Cloudflare's "Always Online" option allows your website to never be down. Always online caches a static version of your website in the event that your website sever ever goes offline to be displayed to visitors until it can be restored.

 Definition: **A CDN (Content Delivery Network)** is a network of servers around the world that work to improve site speed by serving copies of a website from a server that is more closely located geographically to the person requesting the site.

Caching - If you are using WordPress you can add plugins that will help with speed by creating "caches" of your website. The plugins we recommend are:

+ WP Rocket: Caching and Minification Plugin

Definition: A **cache** is a temporary storage area. For example, when you visit a web page, a copy of the web page's content is saved to your computer's hard drive stored on your hard disk in a cache subdirectory under the directory for your browser. for faster repeated viewing.

 Definition: **Minification** is the programming process of reducing the amount of code on your web page. If you have unused CSS (Cascading Style Sheets) on your webpage or Javascript that can be removed, do it.

....

"We want Google to be the third half of your brain."

- SERGEY BRIN

(Co-founder of Google)

....

Optimizing Your Images -

+ WP Smush: This will compress your images to a smaller file size for faster load times
+ Use https://compressor.io to compress png & jpg images.
+ Your filenames must be keyword optimized.
   By default most people name their images as:
   "image-001.jpg." Intentionally you should name your images as:"tulsa-mens-haircuts-image-001.jpg"
+ Alt Tags - Customized descriptive text for ALL images must be added.

Page Optimization - This is where you tell Google what your website and each page is about. If you are using a WordPress website, you can install the Yoast plugin and fill out the following:

+ Meta Description + Focus Keyword (Meta Keywords)
+ Keyword Density (Number of times your keyword is used on the page.)
+ Sitemaps
+ HTML Sitemap
   » Dynamically or statically created index of pages on your website, to improve visitor experience
+ XML Sitemap

Definition: **XML Sitemap**: A dynamically created index of all pages, posts, & articles on your website that allows search engines to more quickly crawl and index the content on your site.

Submitting Your Site to Google:

Once you have built your website to be Google search engine compliant and overall search engine friendly, it is imperative that you must then submit your website to Google to be indexed (sorted, ranked and rated) via the Google Search Console. However, as a general rule you don't want to submit your website to Google on a (daily, weekly or monthly basis). Allow Google to do their thing and allow it to naturally index, crawl and rank your website over time. Over the past 12 years we have found that the businesses that submit their website to Google on a weekly and monthly basis do not rank higher as a result of submitting every week.

Continually Run a Site Audit and Fix the Errors you find:

We recommend using SEMRush.com and setting up a monthly website audit. Google is never done updating so, you too can never be done updating and optimizing your website. Here is a list of common site errors that we find with websites:

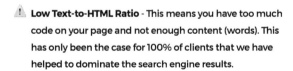 **Low Text-to-HTML Ratio** - This means you have too much code on your page and not enough content (words). This has only been the case for 100% of clients that we have helped to dominate the search engine results.

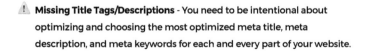 **Missing Title Tags/Descriptions** - You need to be intentional about optimizing and choosing the most optimized meta title, meta description, and meta keywords for each and every part of your website.

⚠ **Duplicate Content - <u>THIS IS A HUGE ISSUE!</u>** You cannot ever duplicate anything. EVER. This goes for Title tags, descriptions, and actual content. You **<u>MUST create ORIGINAL CONTENT</u> on every part of your website**.

⚠ **Missing SSL (Secure Socket Layer)** - You can purchase this from GoDaddy.com

⚠ **Missing ALT Tags** - This is where your images should be labeled and named so that Google knows what the image is all about.

⚠ **Duplicate H1 and Title Tags** - Your H1 heading must be different than your title tag. See chapter 13: *"Fixing Errors"* to learn how to fix these errors and more.

Definition: **Canonical Rules** - When referring to programming, canonical means conforming to well-established patterns or rules. The term is typically used to describe whether or not a programming interface follows the already established standards. You don't want to build a bizarre website that Google does not understand and thus, won't rank high in search engine results unless you hate money.

Fun Fact: Although Steve Jobs completely copied the mouse that was originally created by Xerox, you cannot duplicate content from other websites.

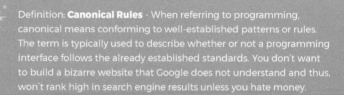

SIDE TIP FOR SEO SUCCESS

"IF YOU EVER GET TEMPTED TO DUPLICATE CONTENT YOU MUST REMEMBER THAT GOOGLE WILL QUICKLY ELIMINATE YOUR WEBSITE FROM THE SEARCH ENGINES."

CLAY CLARK
(Google Certified Specialist)

NOTABLE QUOTABLE

"If you can't explain it simply, you don't understand it well enough."

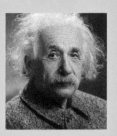

- ALBERT EINSTEIN

(The famous German-born theoretical physicist who saved America by encouraging America's leaders to get serious about creating a nuclear weapon before the Germans did.)

If you get lost or don't understand what we are teaching, please do not hesitate to schedule a time for a member of our team to audit your website at ThrivetimeShow.com/Website.

1984, Palo Alto Research Center (currently owned by Xerox)

OH, NO PROBLEM... NOW IF YOU FOLLOW ME THIS WAY, YOU WILL SEE OUR WONDERFUL COLLECTION OF CAT POSTERS.

THANKS, DAN INGALLS FOR SHOWING ME AROUND THIS FINE FACILITY.

"IF YOU WANT TO SAVE YOURSELF A BUNCH OF TIME, IT IS ALWAYS EASIER TO BE A PIRATE THAN A PIONEER."
- CLAY CLARK, FOUNDER OF THRIVE15

"Ideas are easy. Implementation is hard."
- GUY KAWASAKI

(The iconic New York Times best-selling author, former key Apple employee, venture capitalist, and the chief product evangelist for both Canva and Mercedes Benz)

```html
<header class="chapter-title">
        <p>CHAPTER 5</p>
        <h1>
```

CREATE A GOOGLE MOBILE COMPLIANT WEBSITE

```html
        </h1>

</header>
                        <style>
                            #page-background{
                                background-color: #F4B400;
                            }
                                .chapter-title p{
                                    text-transform: uppercase;
                                    color: white;
                                    font-family: 'Proxima Nova ';
                                    font-weight: 600;
                                }

                                .chapter-title h1{
                                    text-transform: uppercase;
                                    color: white;
                                    font-family: 'Proxima Nova',
                                    font-weight: 900;
                                }
                        </style>
```

Create a Google Mobile Compliant Website.

Your website must meet Google's mobile search compliance rules or you will lose. One of the biggest mistakes you can make when it comes to optimizing your website is to fail to optimize your website for mobile since, according to Forbes, it's estimated that 57% of all online U.S. traffic actually comes from smartphones and tablets. We realize that you might not like all of these rules, but because our good friends at Google are in charge, you'll have to take up your arguments with Larry Page or Sergey Brin (the co-founders of Google). If you want to check the current mobile compliance of your existing website, visit: https://www.google.com/webmasters/tools/mobile-friendly/

If you will optimize your website to make your website comply to Google's standards and rules, your life will improve.

....

"Make something people want. "

- PAUL GRAHAM

(The man behind the success of AirBNB, Dropbox, Reddit, etc.)

....

NOTABLE QUOTABLE

"Anyone who stops learning is old, whether at twenty or eighty. Anyone who keeps learning stays young. The greatest thing in life is to keep your mind young."

- HENRY FORD

(The legendary entrepreneur and the founder of Ford Motor Company.)

NOTABLE QUOTABLE

"Make something people want."

-PAUL GRAHAM

(The founder of Via Web and
the man behind Y-Combinator,
Dropbox, Reddit, AirBnB, etc.)

SUCCESS STORIES

"Before we started working with Clay, we might have eight evaluation lessons in a month. Maybe one or two in a week. But now, at this point, we have eight this week. Eight evaluation lessons this week. Just tomorrow, we have five evaluation lessons and our schedule is getting so packed out that we're borderline running out of room to even to schedule more evaluation lessons, which is why they are also helping us duplicate what I'm able to do in getting other coaches involved in the hiring process and gets into a lot of other levels of things that we are currently working on."

- LEVI NICKSON

(The founder of Tumble Smart
- See his success at TumbleSmart.com)

SUCCESS STORIES

"We're the largest basketball facility in the three or four state area. We have people that call us from all over Oklahoma because of our website. My time has been freed up tremendously because I'm not involved in all the little things. Clay's coaching just streamlines your business so it's not taking just all of your time away from your family. As a business owner if you allow your business to eat you up well it's not really worth it. You've got to have a value of life as well. We wouldn't be where we're at today without Clay Clark."

- DON CALVERT

(Founder of Score Basketball -
See his success at ScoreBBall.com)

NOTABLE QUOTABLE

"If you never want to be criticized for goodness sake, don't do anything new."

- JEFF BEZOS
(The founder of Amazon.com)

"I would like to see anyone be able to achieve their dreams, and that's what this organization does."

- SERGEY BRIN
(Co-founder of Google)

"EVERYTHING ELSE BECOMES UNNECESSARY IN A BUSINESS IF NOBODY SELLS ANYTHING."
- CLAY CLARK

CHAPTER 6

CREATE AND OPTIMIZE YOUR GOOGLE MY BUSINESS CCOUNT

*Example of a
Google My Business listing*

Create and Optimize Your Google My Business Account

Have you ever used your phone to search for a restaurant when you were out of town? Have you noticed that the local business listings that pop up at the top of Google search results for certain terms include user reviews and a number of stars appearing near the listing itself? Usually you can see the business' phone number and address there as well. Well that, is a Google My Business Account. OPTIMIZING YOUR GOOGLE MY BUSINESS ACCOUNT HAS THE POTENTIAL TO LITERALLY DOUBLE YOUR INCOME.

We have worked with countless business owners from nearly every field and industry imaginable (apothecary pharmacies, chiropractors, dentists, fitness companies, lawyers, manufacturers, professional sports teams, and many more) who have been able to literally double the number of inbound calls and leads they were receiving simply by optimizing their Google My Business Account.

YOU MUST OPTIMIZE YOUR GOOGLE MY BUSINESS ACCOUNT AS SOON AS POSSIBLE. In order to get your company to show up

> "The Thrive Program took over our marketing account a little over a month ago and it has worked on increasing our presence on Google. It has been overwhelming, the response that we have had. They have been amazing in getting our presence on Google out there."
>
> - Bridgett (Rescue Heat and Air) - See their success at https://rescueheatandair.com/

in search engine results and to begin gathering those reviews so that you can show up prominently on Google Maps, you will need to optimize your Google My Business account which you can do by going to Business.Google.Com. You can also type in "Google My Business" in the Google search field, follow the link and then completely fill out every area of the form in order to have the most robust Google profile. During this step, you will have to provide a real physical address to verify that you are a real business.

If you get stuck while attempting to do this, you will not be the first human on the planet who has ever done so. Just fill out the form at Thrivetimeshow.com/Website and we will walk you through the process. Why? Because your life matters and we sincerely desire to help you.

While optimizing Your Google My Business account, make sure you include the following:

Confirm that your physical business address is both correct and consistent. If you are operating a home-based business, we recommend that you get a month-to-month office space that provides you with a business mailbox. We realize that this seems blatantly obvious, however it is CRITICAL that your address remains consistent because of the way Google has set up the local search feature. You need to write your address the exact same way every time, because Google cares about this stuff when ranking websites; therefore, we need to care about this stuff. As an example, use "Ave." or "Avenue" (pick one and stick with it). Use the EXACT SAME ADDRESS every time you set up an online address listing for your company on the Internet on websites like YellowPages.com, YEXT, Groupon, Moz, Axciom, InfoGroup, Factual, InsiderPages, Neustar, and the like. Failure to be accurate and consistent will negatively impact your overall ranking in Google's search engine results. When I teach at workshops and other speaking events, some raise their hands right here and say, "But why does Google make you do that?" I typically respond with, "I don't make Google's rules. My game is to learn them and use them to generate copious amounts of money as a result of adhering to them."

"I've paid thousands of dollars to marketing businesses, online marketing businesses, all these different types of businesses, Valpak, all this different stuff. And none of it's ever really done anything for me. But in the last three months, I have made years and leaps forward into the future with my own business because now I'm getting all the leads I need. I have the opportunity to do what I like doing and that is closing deals and I'm also developing my business."

\- John Carter
(Founder of John Carter Bathrooms)

Verify that your hours of business are accurate. Many people now use Google to search for everything and they blindly trust Google to be right about everything. Think about how much money you could be losing if your Google listing says that you are closed during hours when, in fact, you are open. Unfortunately, most businesses discover that their hours are listed incorrectly when they go through this checklist.

Verify that your business is listed in the correct category. For most business owners like you, choosing the category that you are in is not confusing. As an example, if you serve food and you are a restaurant, you would obviously choose to be listed in the "restaurant" category. However, for industries such as public relations, marketing and advertising, you may need to put some thought into determining which category will generate the most calls to your business. You don't want to be oddly missing from Google search results in a business category that you should be dominating, that reflects your core business. Unfortunately, when diligent people like you take the time to audit their Google My Business listing, they often find that their business categories are incorrectly set up. Recently, we worked with a mortgage broker whose business was incorrectly listed under the wrong category. You can imagine that this had a devastating impact on the number of inbound calls he was receiving. Add at least three to five paragraphs of really good content about your business. In this description, make sure to include the name of the local city you are in and how your company can uniquely solve the problems of your ideal and likely buyers. If you get stuck here, please fill out the form at ThrivetimeShow.com/Website and we will help you.

Add as many high quality photos of your business, your checkout area, your offices, and your products and services as Google will allow. Photos really do make a huge impact. In fact, the majority of Internet users today tend to gravitate towards websites that are filled with beautiful images and videos. At the time of this writing, we are managing the online marketing campaigns for hundreds of business owners just like you. These business owners are always blown away when we show them their weekly website traffic analysis and they see for themselves how their website's visitors explore their website. Well over 80% of the people who visit a website do so using their mobile phone, and they tend to scroll up and down the website rapidly.

> Bonus Note - Save your images as your keyword that you are trying to rank for separated by hyphens. Going back to our JohnKnowsDogs. com example, if our keyword was "San Diego Dog Training" you would save each image as San-Diego-dog-training-1.jpeg. Add a different number for each image saved, thus the next image would be saved as San-Diego-dog-training-2.jpeg

Website visitors are mainly searching for compelling photos, videos and a phone number to call. Most business owners fail on this step because they upload poor quality photos to their Google My Business listing. Doing this gives the impression that you are either a hillbilly or the owner of a poorly run business. Although people shouldn't judge us, they do.

Consider adding a 360-degree view or a virtual tour of your business. If you've ever used Google maps, you are undoubtedly familiar with the feature known as "street view." When you click this view, you can walk around the street and actually get a 360° view of a neighborhood, street, or area. Although this is as disturbing as it is great, many consumers prefer to take a 360° virtual tour of your business before deciding whether or not to engage with your business. If you are going to add this feature, you want to do it right. Find a Google trusted photographer at www. google.com/Streetview/contact-tools.

Write a solid, engaging, and complete introduction to your business. This is the section where you describe your beautiful business. During this section of your listing, you should include the carefully selected keywords you are focused on optimizing. For instance, if you are a Tulsa-based orthodontist, you would want to focus on including the keyword phrases "Tulsa Orthodontist, Orthodontists Tulsa, or Orthodontists in Tulsa."

Include the types of payment that you accept. You must be thorough when filling out your Google My Business account, even if it seems to be a massive waste of time. Believe me, it is not. If two businesses are equally matched, the Google My Business listing that is the most complete and most optimized will win.

SUCCESS STORIES 🏆

"Since we implemented the system we now have more money in the bank than we've ever had."

- DAVE & TRICIA RICH

(Pappagallos Pizza - See their success at Pappagallos.com)

* Note: in the past 18 months, Dave and Tricia have grown their beach-front pizzeria by 35%.

"You must decide to push yourself and to kick your own a@$ because nobody else is going to do it."

- CLAY CLARK

NOTABLE QUOTABLE

"Waiting for perfect is never as smart as making progress."

- SETH GODIN

(The best-selling author of 18+ books, and the man who sold his company, Yoyodyne to Yahoo! for $30 million. Seth has been a guest on the *Thrivetime Show Podcast*.)

"THIS PRODUCT IS SO GOOD, IT WILL SELL ITSELF."
— SOMEONE STUPID

<header class="chapter-title">

    <p>CHAPTER 7 </p>
    <h1>

GATHER OBJECTIVE GOOGLE REVIEWS FROM YOUR CURRENT & PREVIOUS CUSTOMERS

    </h1>

</header>
                        <style>
                            #page-background{
                                background-color: #0F9D58;
                            }
                                .chapter-title p{
                                    text-transform: uppercase;
                                    color: white;
                                    font-family: 'Proxima Nova ';
                                    font-weight: 600;

                                }

                                .chapter-title h1{
                                    text-transform: uppercase;
                                    color: white;
                                    font-family: 'Proxima Nova';
                                    font-weight: 900;

                                }
                        </style>

Gather Objective Google Reviews from Your Current & Previous Customers

Google has decided to put the most optimized registered local business with the most "authentic" positive reviews at or near the top of Google search engine results. This means that not only must you properly optimize your local Google business listing, but we must also start being very proactive about wowing. Wowing your customers is the right thing to do every day and it will make it significantly easier to gather some powerful, real, and objective reviews. You cannot afford to sit back and wait for Google reviews to come to you. Go get those reviews. Unlike our good friends at Yelp, who actually penalize business owners for asking for reviews (don't get us started), our buddies at Google allow us to ask our customers for reviews. This is great because once you have the most complete Google My Business account and the most reviews in your area, you will climb to the top of Google search results quickly.

NOTABLE QUOTABLE

"Always deliver more than expected.

- LARRY PAGE
(The Co-founder of Google)

Most business owners fail here by passively waiting for their customers to provide them with reviews and acting as though the negative reviews that have been written don't impact the buying decisions of potential customers. In this current time anonymous reviews can decrease your sales.

The trolls can quickly gain control, so you must proactively e-mail and ask your happy customers to write a review about your business. Most business owners will, by default, lose when it comes to the search engine optimization game. Most people will not typically go out of their way to request objective reviews from their ideal and likely buyers because consciously or subconsciously, they are afraid of rejection.

If you are not proactive about asking for objective reviews from your current or former customers, you will wake up one morning and discover that you have four negative reviews and no positive reviews, because, by default, the anonymous trolls are in control. After working with thousands of businesses all over the planet, we have come to realize that (without being proactive about asking for objective reviews from your customers), by default, you will receive nearly entirely negative reviews.

We want to add this quick note. In nearly every market on the planet, we find that local business owners have to deal with disgruntled ex-employees, ex-spouses, competitors, and irate customers who are impossible to satisfy. Weak a@#! people who are not good at communicating their grievances directly to companies love to leave you and your business bad reviews because it's their passive-aggressive way to be bold, while also remaining weak and hiding behind a screen or a bogus and anonymous username. Nothing is more weak than leaving a business a bad review from an anonymous user account like superfresh227@gmail.com.

You must embrace the truth that the trolls will be the only people writing reviews about your business if you are not intentional about gathering positive Google reviews.

You must respond to the negative reviews in a politically correct way because we now live in a world where political correctness matters 10 times more than actual correctness. We realize that you are not an idiot and that you weren't born yesterday, but we want to make sure that you fully understand this concept. If handled correctly, a negative review can actually provide you with an opportunity to improve the quality of your business and earn the loyalty of both current and potential customers who are watching to see how you will respond to those negative reviews.

If you come across as an irate business owner and personally attack everyone who gives you anything less than a five-star review, this is not good. Most business owners screw up this step by responding poorly to negative reviews. Respond kindly and you will come out ahead. To bring some clarity to what we just talked about, we have included a screenshot of a typical Google search listing on the next page.

DEEP THOUGHTS FROM THE DEVIL'S ADVOCATE

Q: "WHAT IF I DON'T WANT TO ASK PEOPLE TO WRITE REVIEWS AND I JUST WANT THEM TO COME ABOUT ORGANICALLY?"

A: "YOU WILL BE POOR!"

CLAY CLARK
(Google Certified Specialist)

tulsa men's haircuts   🎤   🔍

All   Images   Maps   News   Shopping   More   Settings   Tools

About 321,000 results (0.67 seconds)

Tulsa's Newest Men's Salon | Affordable Men's Haircuts

Ad www.knockoutsriverside.com/ ▾

Come experience Knockouts! We cater specifically to **men**. We offer: **Haircuts**, Beard Trimming,
Facials, Waxing, coloring & more. Save $5 on your first visit. **Men's** Facials. **Men's** Waxing. Affordable
Man Pampering.

Rating ▾   Hours ▾   Sort by ▾

Elephant In The Room Men's Grooming Lounge

4.8 ★★★★★ (1,144) · Barber shop   🌐   ◈
7.5 mi · Tulsa, OK · (918) 877-2219
Open · Closes 8PM   WEBSITE   DIRECTIONS
👤 "This is the best place in Tulsa to get a **haircut**. It's not just a **haircut**, ..."

Elephant in the Room Men's Grooming Lounge of Tul...

4.9 ★★★★★ (1,049) · Barber shop   🌐   ◈
2.3 mi · Tulsa, OK · (918) 877-2219
Open · Closes 8PM   WEBSITE   DIRECTIONS

Elephant in the Room of Broken Arrow Men's Haircuts

4.9 ★★★★★ (1,029) · Barber shop   🌐   ◈
10.5 mi · Broken Arrow, OK · (918) 877-2219
Open · Closes 8PM   WEBSITE   DIRECTIONS

≡ More places

Top 10 Best Mens Haircut in Tulsa, OK - Last Updated June 2019 - Yelp

https://www.yelp.com/search?find_desc=Mens+Haircut&find_loc=Tulsa%2C+OK ▾

King's Den Hairstyling. 25 reviews. $$Barbers, **Men's** Hair Salons. **Tulsa Men's** Shop. 12 reviews.
$$Barbers, Eyebrow Services. Blades Barbering. 4 reviews. $Barbers. Raw Elements Salon. 22
reviews. Hair Worx. 4 reviews. Fords Barber Shop. 13 reviews. Humble Barber. 1 review. Boardroom
Salon For **Men** - **Tulsa**. 5 reviews.

You or a member of your team must invest the time to call, text, and email every customer you know who has anything favorable to say about your business and ask them to write a review. Choosing not to do this is committing marketing suicide, which, unfortunately, we have watched many business owners do over the years. Google has stated repeatedly that you are not allowed to pay people to write favorable reviews, so don't pay people who aren't customers to write you favorable reviews. For the sake of repetition, just call, text, and email every customer you know who has anything positive to say about your business and ask them to write an objective review about your business.

SUCCESS STORIES 🏆

"Last August we had 114 new patients compared to this August, we had 180 new patients. And it's just at the end of the month, when you count that up, you just can't deny what an impact that Clay's new marketing approach has had on our office. In June last year we had 85 new patients. In June this year, we had 126 new patients. It's just astounding. Before, we were trying to implement our ideas, but we didn't have access to a videographer, a photographer, a website designer, search engine optimizer. Through our new digital marketing plan, we have seen a market increase in the number of new patients that we're seeing every month, year over year. Our average is running about 40 to 42% increase, month over month, year over year."

- DR. APRIL LAI

(Partner with Morrow, Lai and Kitterman Dentistry - See her success at MLKDentistry.com)

"The Ultimate Google Maps" Checklist.

If you own a business, getting your Google map to rank highly in the is VITALLY important so we are going to break down the specific steps you need to take in order to do this.

WHAT IS A GOOGLE MAP?

When you Google anything (for this example we will Google "Men's Haircuts Tulsa"), you will see the Google maps "3-Pack" where Elephant in the Room comes up for 2 of our locations and this is BEFORE the organic listings in part because we have far and away the most objective Google reviews.

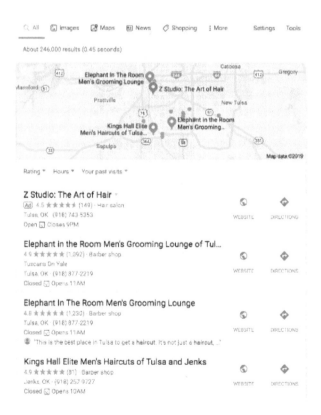

____Step 1: Claim and verify your Google business listing

Elephant In The Room Oklahoma City Men's Haircuts

| Website | Directions | Save |

5.0 ★★★★★ 532 Google reviews

Barber shop in Oklahoma City, Oklahoma

Address: 5701 N Western Ave, Oklahoma City, OK 73118

Go to business.google.com and click "manage now" and follow the prompts. It is important to fill out every single section in its entirety to create and complete your business listing. Make sure to fill out as many categories that apply to your business and that they are as closely related to your business as possible. Also, make sure to have your correct phone number and website filled out. I cannot tell you how many times we see the wrong phone number or URL in their Google business listing. Make sure to have the business description fully filled out. This is an opportunity to set your company apart from others. Make sure to have this filled out to highlight the services you offer that match with the business categories you selected above.

Upload photos, videos, and/or a 360 degree virtual tour. A virtual tour is a great way to show potential customers the experience they can expect, photos (make sure they look good!!) show customers what it looks like, and video testimonials can be uploaded to share previous customers experiences which leads to the next point.

BONUS NOTE: GEOTAG YOUR PHOTOS.

This is nerd speak for basically renaming the core files of the photo to tell Google where you took the photo so it will match your location. You can do this by going to www.geoimgr.com and following the prompts (You can currently do up to 5 photos a day for free).
If you do not claim your Google My Business listing, it doesn't mean that you don't have one. It can be created based on past customers and so by verifying it, you can ensure that you are in control of the information that is being shared online about you. Getting on the first page of Google for
organic listings can be a very long and costly undertaking but claiming your Google listing is free and can help you start to rank on page 1 and to start seeing inbound leads flowing into your website. This is something that you can do immediately to start seeing huge increases in sales and leads. Stop whatever you are doing and go claim that free Google my Business listing.

____**Step 2**: Optimize, Optimize, Optimize

MAKE SURE YOUR MAP AND WEBSITE MATCH!

We stated this earlier but it deserves repeating, Google wants everything to match. It can be very confusing when you go to a Google My Business listing with one address but the website has a different one. You want your Name, Phone number, Address, and Website URL to all match! People in the industry call this NAP but we refuse to use acronyms (see Elon Musk's take on these). Google wants everything to be the same or consistent on everything so it is very important to have your Name, Address, and Phone number on your Google Map EXACTLY THE SAME as what is on your website. The Name of your business, the Address of your business, and the Phone number have to be readily available and visible on your website.

EMBED YOUR MAP ON YOUR WEBSITE
(WHERE IT DOES NOT IMPEDE USER EXPERIENCE)

Google likes it when you use their products thus, we should use their products. This comes with a caveat though because too many times we will see a Google map get embedded on a page and when that website page converts to mobile, you cannot navigate around it. Make sure that the map is in a good place that will not frustrate the user.

Set up Local Schema

We talk about schema throughout the book but this is specific to your local business. For help, reach out to us at Thrivetimeshow.com/website and we will send you a sample code for you to add to your website (for the nerds out there, it is before the </head> tag)

 Definition - **Schema** is microdata that you can add to your HTML to improve the way search engines read and represent your page in SERPs.

___**Step 3:** Gather Citations

A citation is another website or third-party vendor that mentions your "NAP" (name, address, and phone number) on their site. Examples of these would be:

» YP.com (Online Yellow
» Yelp!
» Yahoo
» Whitepages
» Foursquare
» Bing
» Mapquest
» Superpages
» Local.com
» Citysearch
» Credibility.com
» Localpages.com
» GoLocal247
» AroundMe
» YellowPageCity.com
» Etc

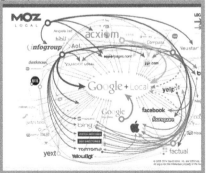

You can go to each of these websites and set up an account manually (THE INFORMATION MUST MATCH YOUR GOOGLE MY BUSINESS LISTING EXACTLY) or you can use a company such as Yext.com to create them all for you, for a fee of course. However, when you setup accounts with Bing, Yelp, and Yellow Pages you now must become very proactive about gathering objective reviews form your current and former clients on each and every listing that you sign up.

____**Step 4:** Gather Objective Reviews

Gathering consistent and objective reviews is super important, for your Google my business ranking and also for to convince potential customers you are credible. How many times have you or someone you know chosen to go to a certain place due to the reviews? Make sure you are intentional about getting objective reviews from your customers. Make this a focus of you and your entire team to get a review from everyone that uses your products or services. Never stop gathering objective reviews.

____**Step 5:** Guest Posting / Getting People to Link to You

Guest posting is a powerful way to earn a backlink to your website (we talk about this in another area of the book) but also for your Google map. If you can anchor text your keyword ie. "Tulsa men's haircuts" and have it link to your Google my business page, this helps you rank higher, faster. The hard part about guest posting is creating the content that people actually want to use on their site.

Getting high quality websites to link to your Google my business listing that have higher "authority rank" then you can also be very helpful but also can be expensive.

For instance, having your name, address, and phone number listed on websites such as the Chamber of Commerce website, or a local community directory is powerful. However, literally convincing another business or organization to link back to you will require much persuasion on your part. Make sure they do not include a "no-follow" link though (social media does) because that is not helpful because it is telling Google to not follow that link back to you.

 A **no follow link** is a link that does not count as a point in the page's favor, does not boost PageRank, and doesn't help a page's placement in the SERPs. No follow links get no love. Theirs is a sad and lonely life. The nofollow tag is basically a notice sign for search engines saying "don't count this."

```
108    rel="nofollow">add one</a> <span class="bracket">}</span></p>
109                              </div>
110                      <dl id="comment_list">
111                          <dt class="comment even thread-even depth-1" id="comment-29
112                              <span class="comment_num"><a href="#comment-293043"
       rel="nofollow">1</a></span>
113                              <span class="comment_author">amra</span> <span clas
114                          </dt>
115                          <dd class="comment even thread-even depth-1">
116                              <div class="format_text" id="comment-body-293043">
117    <p>i wish i could read all day&#8230;</p>
118                              </div>
119                          </dd>
120                          <dt class="comment odd alt thread-odd thread-alt depth-1" i
121                              <span class="comment_num"><a href="#comment-293044"
       rel="nofollow">2</a></span>
```

"Not having a clear goal leads to death by a thousand compromises."

- MARK PINCUS
(The founder of Zynga)
. . . .

"You have to make every single detail perfect and you have to limit the number of details to perfect."

- JACK DORSEY
(The founder and CEO of Twitter and the founder and CEO of Square)
. . . .

CHAPTER 8

CREATE THE MOST RELEVANT & KEYWORD-RICH ORIGINAL CONTENT POSSIBLE

Create the Most Relevant and Keyword-Rich Original Content Possible

Perhaps you've been online searching the phrase "free range chickens" or the word "dog" or the name "Ryan Tedder" and you've noticed Wikipedia's page at or near the top of nearly every Internet search you perform. Perhaps you think it's odd that we would use the phrase "free range chickens" as an example...but we move on.... Have you ever asked yourself why our good friends at Wikipedia are nearly always near the top of Google search results? It's because Wikipedia follows nearly every one of Google's search engine compliance rules and they have more relevant and original HTML text content than anyone else about most subjects.

 Definition Magician: **(HTML) Hypertext Markup Language** - A standardized system for tagging text files to achieve font, color, graphic, and hyperlink effects on World Wide Web pages. This markup is what tells the Internet browser how to show website images and words to the user.

....

"Always deliver more than expected."
LARRY PAGE
(Co-founder of Google)
....

So how do you generate more content than nearly anyone else about a given subject? You must write your content following these six steps if you ever plan to get to the top of Google search results during your living years (after you are dead, we're not sure that you will care if you are at the top in Google search results anymore).

Step 1:___Buy the Nuance Dragon Headset, which allows you to turn your talk into text. Basically, this device transcribes the words you speak into pages of text. Remember, you must have more original and keyword rich text on your website than your competition. This headset makes generating that content a little bit easier (for most people) since you can just talk and allow the headset and your computer do the rest of the work. You can buy this device on Amazon or at nuance.com. If you don't fully understand what we are saying here, book your tickets to attend one of our 2-day interactive business workshops and we'll schedule time to teach you these super moves. Buy your tickets today at ThrivetimeShow.com.

Step 2:___Commit to writing more relevant content than any of your competitors about the search term results that you are focused on winning. When you are writing this content, make sure that you reference the keyword that you are focused on winning such as "Tulsa orthodontists" six times per 1,000 words. Here is where the headset mentioned in Step 1 comes into play. Typically, 10 minutes of speaking will produce approximately 1,000 words of original relevant content. Google wants every page of your website to contain at least 350 words of content, thus you want to over-deliver and wow them by creating 1,000 words of content per page. **Do not do more.** This is considered "Keyword Stuffing."

Why, you ask? Google is the boss and that is what they want, so that is what we shall do. In order to actually generate this content, you must set aside specific time in your schedule to get this done. In Clay's own core businesses, he pays a team of people to write this type of content for his companies every day. Yes, every day. You must have more original, relevant, and keyword-rich content than your competition if you want to win. To figure out how many pages of original content your competition has, you can add "site:" to the beginning of the URL to see.

> Example site:johnknowsdogs.com *shows he has 67 pages of*
> *original and relevant content being indexed by Google.*

If you implement all of the action steps that we are teaching and if you have twice as many 1,000 word pages of original and relevant content that are all about the single keyword phrase "San Diego Dog Training," we will win.

site:johnknowsdogs.com

All   Images   News   Shopping   Maps   More   Settings   Tools

About 67 results (0.23 seconds) ← THE TOTAL NUMBER OF INDEXED PAGES THAT GOOGLE IS COUNTING AS OF THE TIME OF THIS SEARCH.

Try Google Search Console
www.google.com/webmasters/
Do you own **johnknowsdogs.com**? Get indexing and ranking data from Google.

San Diego Dog Trainer and Expert Canine Behaviorist | John's Natural ...
www.johnknowsdogs.com/ ▾
San Diego's most popular, and Voted the BEST, dog trainer, John's Natural Dog Training Company. For 25 years Trainer John Rubin is San Diego's Dog ...

San Diego's John's Natural Dog Training | Classes and Private Training
www.johnknowsdogs.com/services.htm ▾
For an even more customizable and comprehensive training experience, we offer our K9 Personal Trainer Program. ... We offer Puppy Socialization, Beginner, Intermediate, Advanced, and Canine Good Citizen Classes. ... Our Most Requested Dog Obedience Training Program!

Step 3:___Block out a specific time and place every day to write your content. You have to be intentional about this. Don't get nefarious here. Don't look for shortcuts or start copying text from other websites to save time. Google is a multi-billion-dollar company that invests countless dollars annually into catching businesses that are simply copying text from their websites. Years ago, a homebuilder reached out to us to help him grow his business and increase the overall effectiveness of his marketing. He asked us to look into why his website was perpetually found at the bottom of Google search results or even not found at all.

After simply using the free tool that is available at http://www.copyscape.com/duplicate-content/, we found our answer. Much to his dismay, we showed him that his website was an exact replica of another website for a business located in the Northeastern United States. The web development company he hired to build his website simply copied the text from another homebuilder's website.

NOTABLE QUOTABLE

"If you cannot do great things, do small things in a great way."

- **NAPOLEON HILL**
(Best-selling author of Think & Grow Rich)

The website development company apparently assumed he would never check whether his copy was original or not, and they were right. We need to be much wiser about how content is created for our websites. Any time that we allow anyone to write content for our websites, we must ensure that your teammates are not sabotaging your website by copying text. Be careful and remember that, according to the U.S. Chamber of Commerce, 75% of U.S. employees steal from the workplace and most do so repeatedly.

You can check for duplicate content by using the free tool at copyscape.com/duplicate-content/. If you find yourself in the same boat as our homebuilder friend and your website has been penalized by Google for duplicate content issues, fill out the form at ThrivetimeShow.com/Website so that we can help you to get back in good standing with Google.

NOTABLE QUOTABLE

"As I grow older I pay less attention to what men say. I just watch what they do."

- ANDREW CARNEGIE

(A man who started working at a cotton mill 12 hours per day for $1.20 per week (which is $35 per week today adjusted for inflation) at the age of 13 to help his family to pay the bills.)

If you ever get the urge to try to save both time and money by reducing the amount of content that you place on each page of your website, please understand that this is not a good idea. Google has a habit of not highly ranking, featuring, or indexing (showing in search results) website pages that do not have at least 350 words of content per page, which is why you must always write 1,000 words of content per page of your website..

If you are writing your own search engine optimization content, you have to move quickly to create massive amounts of content if you are going to beat our competition during your lifetime on planet earth. Because of the volume of work involved, you may choose to hire some people to generate content for your business. Determine a pay scale for the people you will employ to write the content that will allow you to win for your chosen search term. As of 2019, we believe that a pay scale that allows your writers to earn around $15-$25 per hour (writing at a rapid pace) is the right amount. If you disagree, that is fine, but it is important that you use a merit-based pay program for your search engine optimization team or you will be paying your employees to lament about writer's block rather than to write the content you need.

Pay your writers based upon what they do, not based upon what they say they'll do, or you will find yourself paying a member of your team to write 1 article per week by default. We're not exaggerating when we say that we have literally worked with hundreds of business owners who have attempted to pay their search engine optimization content writers either a salary or an hourly wage and in all cases, the quality of the content they generated ranged between horrible, not enough, and non-existent.

When evaluating the pay scale you will offer, remember that the geniuses who run both our federal government and state governments don't know how to balance a budget, because they generate debt on a weekly and monthly basis. Our government simply prints money when they run out, and you can't do this legally. This printing of money (known as fiat currency) decreases the value of our money each year. This is why the cost of living goes up every year. Keep this in mind and raise the amount you pay your people every two to three years to keep up with inflation, because every year your money is worth about 3% less than it was worth last year.

 FUN FACT: In October 1976, the government officially changed the definition of the dollar; references to gold were removed from statutes. From that point on, the international monetary system was made up solely of fiat money. Thus, our U.S. government can now spend money on whatever they want without a budget and whenever they run out of money, they can just print more. Good job, government. Thank you for proving, yet again, that President Reagan was right when he said "The nine most terrifying words in the English language are "I'm from the government and I'm here to help." - President Ronald Reagan

 Definition Magician - **"Fiat currency"** is legal tender whose value is backed by the government that issued it. The U.S. dollar is fiat money, as is the euro and most other major world currencies. This approach differs from money whose value is underpinned by some physical good such as gold or silver commodity.

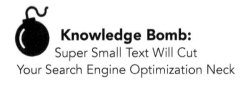 **Knowledge Bomb:**
Super Small Text Will Cut
Your Search Engine Optimization Neck

SUCCESS STORIES 🏆

"In the last 4 months, our internet leads have grown by 12 times!"

- AARON ANTIS

(The marketing director for ShawHomes.com who has sold more than $800 million of homes during his career)

When you attempt to hide your text from search engines you will get hidden from your customers because most search engines will ban your website. In the early days of search engine optimization many web development companies wrote all of the keyword content using white text that they hid because it was pasted at the bottom of websites on top of a white background.

 Definition Magician - A **spider** is a program that visits Web sites and reads their pages and other information in order to create entries for a search engine index. The major search engines on the Web all have such a program, which is also known as a "crawler" or a "bot."

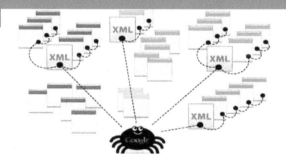

 Fun Fact: Search engines do not like content that is found (buried) more than three clicks from the home page of your website. In fact, more often than not, "spiders" and "bots" will often ignore deep pages on your website. Search engines also do not like pages that are split into "frames" because they hinder the crawling of the "spiders" and "bots."

NOTABLE QUOTABLE

"I do not think that there is any other quality so essential to success of any kind as the quality of perseverance."

- JOHN D. ROCKEFELLER

(A man who had to drop out of Cleveland's Central High School in order to provide much needed income for his mom.)

Bonus Note - When writing articles about the keywords, Google wants you to answer "who, what, when, why, and where." When you Google something you are looking for an answer, thus when writing content you should be answering questions.

Thus, the text was hidden from customers. However, Google has determined that if you are trying to hide your text, you are probably up to something that is less than positive.

Thus, today if you try to hide your text you will find your website quickly disappearing from Google search engine results.

Over time Google has noticed that business people who try

"I'M A GREAT BELIEVER IN LUCK, AND I FIND THE HARDER I WORK, THE MORE I HAVE OF IT."
- THOMAS JEFFERSON
3RD PRESIDENT OF THE USA

- TRANSLATION -
IF YOU TAKE ENOUGH SHOTS YOU WILL EVENTUALLY HIT SOMETHING.

to write text in super small fonts are typically "trying to hide the text" from their website visitors. Thus, don't write content on your website using 2 point font in an attempt to hide your text from users because the search engines will ban you from their search results.

Make Sure That Each Page of Your Website Actually Engages Your Ideal and Likely Buyers (Make Sure Your Website is "Sticky"):

We must make sure that our website actually engages our ideal and likely buyers because it is an epic waste of time to get our ideal and likely buyers to visit our websites if they do not actually become a lead, an inbound call or a prospective client of some type.

Install Lucky Orange

At some point (and as soon as possible) you must install LuckyOrange.com onto your website so that you can actually know what your ideal and likely buyers are doing on your website. It's both creepy and awesome how much you can learn by investing 1 hour per week to look at the data provided by LuckyOrange.com. Using LuckyOrange.com you can actually see where on your website users are clicking on, what they are not clicking on and how they are using or not using your website.

....

"Complaining is not a strategy."
- JEFF BEZOS
(Founder of Amazon.com)
....

SUCCESS STORIES

"We started working with Clay 2 years ago with 600 members at our gym and we just topped 1,800 members. This program literally saved my life."

- LUKE OWENS
(The founder of The Hub Gym - See his success at TheHubGym.com)

- Why are you seeking to increase the amount of sales your business does?
- Why are you desiring to increase your income?

Take a moment and define your 1 year goals for the following areas of your life.

Faith: _____.
_____
Family: _____
_____
Finances: _____.
_____
Friendship: _____
_____
Fitness: _____.
_____
Fun:_____
_____

.

```html
<header class="chapter-title">
    <p>CHAPTER 9</p>
    <h1>
```

GENERATE THE MOST HIGH QUALITY BACKLINKS POSSIBLE

```html
    </h1>
</header>
<style>
    #page-background{
        background-color: #F4B400;
    }
    .chapter-title p{
        text-transform: uppercase;
        color: white;
        font-family: 'Proxima Nova ';
        font-weight: 600;
    }

    .chapter-title h1{
        text-transform: uppercase;
        color: white;
        font-family: 'Proxima Nova';
        font-weight: 900;
    }
</style>
```

Generate the Most High Quality Backlinks Possible

Although this is not as big of a deal as it once was, it can still be helpful. Link building is the action of acquiring hyperlinks from other high ranking websites that link to your own website. Although you cannot control what people do with their websites, you can strongly encourage people to share about your website and add a link from their website to yours. However, before you go out there and devote huge amounts of time to chasing unicorns, leprechauns, and backlinks, you must understand that getting someone to backlink to you is like getting a stranger to allow you to borrow their car. It's tough. A hyperlink from another website to yours is most often referred to as a "backlink." Google and other search engines will count the number of high quality backlinks that you have pointed toward your website as they crawl around the web in their never-ending quest to determine which site should be awarded the top position in their search engine results. No matter what anyone says to you, do not buy cheap backlinks! **Buying backlinks will kill your search engine ranking.**

For backlinks to be most effective, they must include the proper anchor text. Anchor text basically describes to the search engines the overall subject of the website page that is being linked to. Well-written anchor text will always include the main keywords you are focused on winning. You cannot control the words or actions of the other websites that are linking back to you, but in many cases, the individuals running those sites will ask you for a suggestion of what text you would like to have displayed in the backlink.

Let us give you an example:

> *Score Basketball is proud to provide the best Tulsa basketball lessons in the region. For over 30 years, Coach Calvert and his team have provided northeast Oklahoma's most well-known and results-focused Tulsa basketball camps and customized Tulsa basketball coaching experience.*

In this example, "Tulsa basketball lessons" serves as the anchor text. Those are the keywords this business owner is focused on winning. When Google sees that you and I have received a high quality backlink from a website that is using text like this, it celebrates this activity by moving your website up higher and higher up those Google search results.

Although you could spend a nuclear half-life on the Internet researching the various theories of so-called search engine experts, bloggers and academics, we are going to make your life easier by listing for you here the SIX SUPER MOVES that work.

1. **Gather Online Citations for Your Business**
   (Registering your business on 3rd party websites)

2. **Guest Blogging and Podcasting**

3. **Guest Article Writing**

4. **Testimonial Links**

5. **Blog Writing (on your own website)**

NOTABLE QUOTABLE

"Often, the best companies are ones where the product is an extension of the founder's personality."

- NAVAL RAVIKANT
(Founder of AngelList.com)

NOTABLE QUOTABLE

"Action is the real measure of intelligence."

- NAPOLEON HILL

(Best-selling self-help author of *Think and Grow Rich* and the former apprentice of Andrew Carnegie)

Citations 101: A citation is when another website references your business name, phone number, and address as listed on your website. The most common citations come from places that you are probably familiar with: BingPlaces.com, Google.com/business (business.google.com), InsiderPages.com, SuperPages.com, Yelp.com, FourSquare.com, MerchantCircle.com, 411.com, Mapquest.com, and other sites like that. You see, our good friends at Google use citations to help them decide whether or not your business should be considered a relevant entity in their Knowledge Graph. The Google Knowledge Graph is an incredibly large base of knowledge that is used by Google in its never-ending pursuit to improve its already massive search engine results.

YEXT.COM OFFERS AN EFFECTIVE TOOL FOR REGISTERING YOUR WEBSITE WITH 3RD PARTY WEBSITES IN A SCALABLE WAY.

Asking Your Business Network to Link to You

Google's "disturbingly large" semantic search data is being continuously gathered from a variety of sources. As you talk or type into your phone the various items that you are using Google to look for, Google is learning more and more about you so that it can accurately (some say "disturbingly accurately") begin to understand your intent and predict what the most relevant search results should be just for you. The semantic search project is yet another massive project Google has taken on to dramatically enhance the consistency and accuracy of the search results generated for its users. The best tools to speed along the creation of hundreds of high quality citations for your website are Yext.com and Moz.com/Local. These are both paid services that we use when working with our clients and in our own business ventures.

 Guest Blogging and Podcasting: If you are an expert in your field and you are willing to commit the time needed to produce accurate, insightful and helpful content that can be either listened to or read by your ideal and likely buyers, then you should reach out to the various bloggers and podcasters within your niche to see if you can be a guest contributor for their blog or podcast. When you produce a quality piece of content, most bloggers and podcasters will provide a link back to your website from their website, thus generating a high quality and relevant backlink from a trusted source within your industry. For additional trainings on the specifics of how to systematically reach out to the top podcasters and bloggers within your niche, visit www.ThrivetimeShow.com/business-coach-podcast/

 Guest Article Writing: If you love to write or at least have the ability to generate expert and compelling content that your ideal and likely buyers want to read, you should reach out to various online publications to become a guest writer / contributor. Make sure when contributing they offer you a "follow link" & not a "no-follow" (which means it allows Google to follow the link back to your site).

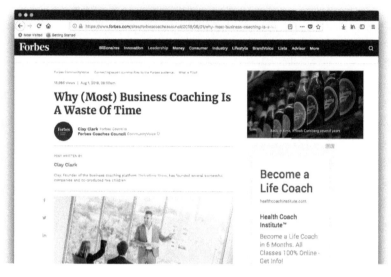

 Testimonial Links: If you have provided an extremely high level of satisfaction to your ideal and likely buyers, you need to begin gathering testimonial links from your clients. Basically, a testimonial link is a backlink to your website that is found within a paragraph that contains a large amount of sincere, relevant information touting your website as a source of wisdom and knowledge. Your customers' websites may contain a page dedicated to explaining how they are proud to partner with great vendors like you. **Consider this example:**

> In Tulsa you can find a large variety of restaurants and bakeries that serve gourmet cookies.
> However, for the best cookies in Tulsa, you need to experience Barbee's Tulsa cookies. Barbee's has delicious cookies of all shapes and sizes and you can even now buy her cookies online. When we need to send our clients a special gift, without reservation we use BarbeeCookies.com and you should too.

Blog Writing (on your own website): If you invest both the time and effort to create quality blogs and articles on your website that actually provide useful or entertaining information, many people will naturally want to share the article then link back to your website. When you write an article that is non-sales oriented, educational, informative, or entertaining, people will begin to link to you quite often.

TO MAKE YOUR LIFE 2% BETTER, WE HAVE PROVIDED A FEW EXAMPLES OF WHAT WE ARE TALKING ABOUT:

01. Articles about topical and hot news issues: Writings about Justin Bieber's most recent attempts to stay clean, Donald Trump saying something polarizing, or Great Britain's decision to leave the European Union as part of the Brexit movement are all examples of this kind of article. Perez Hilton has made a great living writing these kinds of articles.

02. Humorous or Engaging Content: If you are a Jedi Master when it comes to writing funny stories about topics that humans enjoy, then this may just be your super move for generating high quality backlinks. If you recorded a daily video blog or a weekly podcast or wrote a daily blog about an engaging perspective on life, your fans will begin to want to share your content with their friends. As they begin to share, more and more high quality backlinks will pour in. As an example, the good people at WestJet Airlines invested the time, money and energy into creating a video that has been shared some 45 million times to date. You can check out the video at: www.YouTube.com/watch?v=zIElvi2MuEk

03. How-To Guides: When you take the time needed to thoroughly explain how to do something in both an easy and concise way using visuals, videos, text, or infographics, people will naturally begin to share backlinks to your website. The Pioneer Woman (Ree Drummond) is a powerful example of somebody who is now making millions of dollars and generating thousands of backlinks thanks to her powerful How-To Guides. Visit her website at:

thepioneerwoman.com/cooking

04. Top Ten Lists: David Letterman feasted on the power of Top Ten lists during his career as a late night talk show host and you can too. When you write a helpful top ten list related to your industry, people will share it time and time again. Some examples of this are the Top Ten Ways to Be a Better Dad, the Top 10 Ways to Save More Money, and the Top Ten Ways to Properly Feed and Raise Organic Free Range Chickens. For cathartic reasons people will provide the backlinks you need if they find your content to be helpful. As an example, the powerful entrepreneurial podcast, Entrepreneurs On Fire, published a blog post titled, "Top 15 Business Books Recommended by Today's Top Entrepreneurs."

The Entrepreneurs On Fire: "Top 15 business books recommended by today's top entrepreneurs" has been shared 589 times as of the time we are writing this book.

See this blog post by going to:

www.eofire.com/top-15-business-books-recommended-todays-top-entrepreneurs/

05. Helpful Resources: If you and your team (which might consist of you and yourself) are willing to invest the time required to document new research, surveys, case studies, compelling charts, infographics, or interesting graphs, this will also create backlinks to your website over time.

We've employed this tactic ourselves over the years, and we have added hundreds of practical resources, templates, and downloadables for entrepreneurs and business owners like you that can be accessed by only our ThrivetimeShow.com members. These have generated plenty of backlinks for our site. Check out the free and powerful resources we have created for you today at:
www.Thrivetimeshow.com/resources.

06. Asking Your Business Network to Link to You:
Many business relationships are very mutually beneficial, meaning that both parties need each other to be successful. To give you an idea of how this can work, years ago we helped a general family doctor generate nearly 100 high quality backlinks by convincing suppliers, the insurance representatives, the pharmaceutical sales reps, and other people with whom he did business to provide a link on their website to his using the proper anchor text. Why did they do this? They did this because the good doctor agreed to feature them on his on-going podcast and because as his practice grew, many of these vendors benefited as a direct result of his success. The more patients he sees the more supplies he orders, the more prescriptions he writes, and the win-win success goes on and on.

SIDE TIP FOR SEO SUCCESS

SEARCH ENGINE OPTIMIZATION REQUIRES TIME AND NOTHING GETS DONE UNLESS IT GETS SCHEDULED. WHEN WILL YOU SCHEDULE A WEEKLY TIME TO WORK ON YOUR SEARCH ENGINE OPTIMIZATION?

JONATHAN KELLY
(Google Certified Specialist)

NOTABLE QUOTABLE

"Be so good they can't ignore you."

- STEVE MARTIN

(The Emmy and Grammy award-winning playwright, pianist, author, comedian, actor, and banjo player.)

"Patience, persistence and perspiration make an unbeatable combination for success."

- NAPOLEON HILL

(Best-selling author of *Think and Grow Rich*)

SUPER MOVE

The Power of the Disavow:

You cannot help who links to you, but if you notice someone linking to you with a spam backlink or a shady website, you can create a disavow which tells Google that you do not want to be associated with that link.

For help with this and to request an example disavow file, visit

ThrivetimeShow.com/website

You can find out what sites link to you through several different ways:

1. Google Search Console

2. Majestic - Paid website that crawls the web to find links to your site and gives them a quality score.

3. Screaming Frog - Free desktop app

4. SEMRush.com - Links to your website can also be tracked here.

"A goal is a dream with a deadline."

- NAPOLEON HILL

(The best-selling author of all-time before Jack Canfield's *Chicken Soup for the Soul*.)

....

When will you begin to execute the proven systems being taught in this book?

Date: _____

What <u>specific times</u> <u>each week</u> will you block out for search engine optimization?

Date: _____

Time: _____

....

<header class="chapter-title">

<p> CHAPTER 10 </p>

<h1>

HOW TO WRITE ORIGINAL CONTENT

</h1>
</header>

<p>"This chapter could be worth millions to you or it could be worth ABSOLUTELY nothing. It's up to you." - **Clay Clark**</p>

How to Write Original Content

1. H1 TAG PRIORITIZE

(H1 STANDS FOR HEADING 1)

You must include the keyword phrase you are focused on optimizing for within the first sentence of each webpage's content. This text must be in complete sentence form.

DO NOT EVER DUPLICATE H1 text on other pages of your website. Google hates this and thus, we HATE IT TOO.

Do not duplicate the Title Tag with your H1 tag

Example of well written H1 Tag:
Are you looking for the best haircuts in Tulsa?

DEFINITION MAGICIAN: **H1 Text 101:** H1 text is the hypertext markup language element that is used to usually identify the title of an article or page of website content. It's the biggest word on the top of a webpage. If you look above you will see that the word "Dog" on the Wikipedia listing is clearly the biggest word on the page. This is because the word "dog" is the most important keyword focus for this page.

Step 1: Select the Page or Article that you wish to edit

Step 2: Select text that you want to make H1 text and enlarge it using "Heading 1" in the paragraph field

Step 3: Make sure that the H1 text is a complete sentence. *(Find Tulsa Men's Haircuts at the Elephant in the Room.)*

Step 4: Check again to be sure your H1 text is a complete sentence with a subject, verb and a period.

Step 5: Be sure the H1 text is at the top of the page.

2. FILL OUT ARTICLE DESCRIPTION (THIS ISN'T THE META DESCRIPTION)

- Make sure to include a title for all content that you are writing, just like you would if you were writing a college paper.
- Below the actual title of the content on each page, you must write the description. DO NOT EVER DUPLICATE the description text or any text.
- The phone number should appear on the top of every web page where content is being written.

  Example - This article is about how to find a quality men's haircut in Tulsa

  Example - This business coaching blog is about how to create a pro-forma that is usable.

3. KEYWORDS (THIS ISN'T THE META KEYWORDS)

Include the keyword or keyword phrase that you are focusing on six times per 1000 words. The keyword phrase you are focusing on must actually be woven into the article or blog content (see below).

> *Example / Sample Paragraph: At Elephant in the Room Men's Grooming Lounge, we are focused on providing the very best Owasso haircut. In fact, since first opening our doors at 1609 South Boston in the heart of downtown Tulsa, we have been able to grow our business exponentially as a result of focusing relentlessly on providing a premium grooming experience every time. Now as we expand out just to the north of Tulsa, we are excited about bringing the very best Owasso haircut to this rapidly growing city.*

Fun Fact: It should take you approximately an average of 1 hour to physically write 1,000 words of content. Thus if you need to create 400 pages of original, relevant content to beat your competition in the search engine results, you should expect your team to be able to create 400 pages of content in just 400 short hours. ***Do not add more than 6 keywords per 1,000 words as this is considered "keyword stuffing" and Google will greatly penalize you for it**.

4. CONTENT / TEXT

- A minimum of 1,000 words of original high quality content must be created per page on the website you are focused on optimizing.

- Producing 1,000 words of content is equal to spending approximately 10 minutes talking on a talk-to-text Dragon headset or 1 hour spent writing.
- We highly discourage you from attempting to write content needed for your website by typing on every page of your website except for the main pages (the core pages of your website). We would strongly encourage you to use talk-to-text transcription technology like Dragon so that you can save your time, money and sanity. When creating content, make sure to answer the following questions as you talk into the Dragon headset.

1. **Who is this content being written for?**

2. **Who is ideally searching for this content?**

3. **What is this content about?**

4. **Why does this content matter?**

5. **What do you want your reader to do as a result of this content?**

6. **Why are you passionate about this content?**

7. **How is your company different from everybody else in the market?**

8. **What is your company's information? (Phone #)**

As you create content, you want to make sure that it will be scored highly by Google. In order to score highly, you must include synonyms and industry-related jargon to the topic that you are focused on optimizing and you must receive a high readability score.

Content that receives a high READABILITY SCORE from Google will rank higher. Readability scores will be higher if you actually make sense and are saying something of meaning. Include synonyms and other industry related terms in your content.

We highly encourage you to do a Wikipedia search for the keywords that you are focused on optimizing, then write down six words and terms related to the keyword. Focus on weaving these terms into each article that you write.

To increase the quality of the content that you are writing, use proper punctuation. Avoid long run-on sentences. Spell things correctly. Check your work after the article is written. Company names, awards and personal names must be capitalized (Dragon Command 'Caps On')

The content of the article must be relevant to the company and must always be truthful. All articles must be written in "Text Edit" and saved as a .TXT (no Word documents allowed). If you choose to save every file as a Word Document (.docx), you will pay for it later as you are forced to reformat all of the content that you add to the website. When you save a text file as a Word document, it makes the process of uploading the content 30% harder.

After you are done writing, scan the article to make sure that it makes sense. If someone else is writing the content for you, you must check whether content has been copied from another website by using: www.copyscape.com/duplicate-content/.

Also, check for content copied from other pages on your own website using www.siteliner.com.

5. CREATE MORE RELEVANT CONTENT THAN ANYONE IN YOUR NICHE

Step 1: ___Determine how much content your competition has had indexed by Google using this incredible tool: http://freetools.webmasterworld.com/. Click on "Indexed Pages." OR site:URL

Step 2: ___YOU CANNOT EVER DUPLICATE CONTENT. Doing this is like inviting Satan into your life. Google will flag your website for duplicate content and your website will drop like a rock from the search engine results. Check for duplicate content using:

> *https://www.copyscape.com/duplicate-content/*
> *https://siteliner.com/*

Step 3: ___Don't stop writing until you have written more high-quality and original text than your competition. Search around your office for original content that you

As you mentally debate as to whether you will implement the proven systems that you are learning always remember, nobody is going to wake up with a burning desire to buy your products or services if they can't find you and if they don't know you exist.

have written in the past and get that uploaded to your website. Many companies have a gold mine of thousands of pages of transcripts or original content sitting on a computer somewhere. Use it.

6. FEATURED IMAGE (ADD A NEW IMAGE FOR EACH ARTICLE)

Step 1: ___Every image that you add to your website must be optimized. You must own the rights to every image that you add to your website.

At Thrivetimeshow.com, we subscribe to GettyImages.com and IStockPhoto.com so that we can use the massive library of high quality images. Both of these companies have carefully organized and licensed millions of images.

  a. Select a place to put the image.

  b. Click on Add Media.

  c. Click on Upload Image (must be an image that you have the rights to).

  d. Name the image. When you save the image, use dashes, not spaces or underlines.

   Example: owasso-mens-haircuts-haircut-1.jpg.

When you title the image, use the same words, but remove the dashes.

  e. Title the image following this format:

   Example: Owasso Men's Haircut | Shaving Tools
   Example: Business Coaching | Woman in a Coffee Shop

  f. Set the image to medium size.

  g. Set the image to the left side of the page.

SUCCESS STORIES

"It's wife bragging time. (Because I know she won't do it herself...) We started Sprik Realty just over a year ago. Which means 2016 is our first full calendar year. Numbers are in for the year and I couldn't be more proud. With Clay's coaching we are over $23 million in sales for the year!! 2017 is going to be AWESOME!! Congrats Danielle Sprik and all the Sprik Agents. Keep doing what you do."

TIM SPRIK

(Co-founder of Sprik Realty)

Prefer hands-on workshop style learning?

Book your tickets to attend the world's highest and most reviewed workshop today at ThrivetimeShow.com. These workshops only cost $37 to attend if you have purchased a copy of this book.

h. Use the formatting buttons to wrap the text around the image.
i. Name the Alt Text: the same as the Title Image. No description of the image is needed.

 Fun Fact: Getty Images was started by J. Paul Getty, who was named the richest living American by *Fortune* magazine in 1957.

NOTABLE QUOTABLE

"Work like hell. I mean, you just have to put in 80-100 hour weeks every week. This improves the odds of success. If other people are putting in 40 hour work weeks and you're putting in 100 hour work weeks, then even if you're doing the same thing you know that you will achieve in 4 months what it takes them a year to achieve."

- ELON MUSK

(The man behind Telsa, SpaceX, PayPal, SolarCity)

"FACE REALITY AS IT IS, NOT AS IT WAS
OR AS YOU WISH IT TO BE."
– JACK WELCH
FORMER CEO OF GENERAL ELECTRIC

```
<header class="chapter-title">
    <p>
```

CHAPTER 11

```
<h1>
```

UPLOADING ARTICLES / TEXT CONTENT CHECKLIST

```
</h1>
</header>

        <style>
            #page-background{
                background-color: #4285F4;
            }

                .chapter-title p{
                    text-transform: uppercase;
                    color: white;
                    font-family: 'Proxima Nova ';
                    font-weight: 600;
                }

                .chapter-title h1{
                    text-transform: uppercase;
                    color: white;
                    font-family: 'Proxima Nova';
                    font-weight: 900;
                }
        </style>
```

Once you are ready to upload the content that you and your team have written for your website, it is very important that you follow this checklist. Keep a log of uploaded content that includes the following details:

WARNING: DUPLICATE CONTENT IS THE DEVIL

Article Uploaded #: _____

Initials of Uploader: _____

Date of Article Upload: _____

Keyword: _____

1.___ADD CONTENT TO WEBSITE: NO DUPLICATE CONTENT IS ALLOWED.

___Login to website > Choose Posts / Articles

___Copy and paste two 500 word articles into the body (or one 1,000 word article)

___ Set H1 heading, if not automatically created by your WordPress theme.

___Scroll down to the Yoast SEO plugin

2.___FILL OUT META TITLE (REFERRED TO AS THE "SNIPPET EDITOR" IN SEO YOAST)

a. Must not include more than nine words (less than 71 characters)

b. Must include a "vertical bar" |
(located above the return / enter key)

c. Must include the keyword and article title

Example: – Men's Haircuts in Tulsa

Example: – Men's Haircuts in Tulsa I Find Superior Cut

3.___FILL OUT META DESCRIPTION

a. Write content that you want to show up on the actual Google search results.

b. Keep this to two sentences, maximum. Include the keyword in the first sentence.

a. Include the phone number / call to action in the second sentence.

d. This content must fit into the SEO Yoast character rule limit (156 characters).

> *Example: Are you looking for a premium south Tulsa Men's haircut? Call the award-winning Elephant in the Room team at 918-877-2219.*

> *Example: In this article award-winning business coach teaches management with the former EVP of Disney World, Lee Cockerell. Sign up for a free trial today.*

4.___ADD THE ONE "FOCUS KEYWORD"

a. SEO Yoast will ask you to determine one "Focus Keyword" that you are focused on.

b. Choose the "Focus Keyword" for SEO Yoast based upon what keyword phrase the content you are uploading was focused on.

c. The keywords that you list must be included in the actual article.

> *Example - Business Coaching*

5.___ADD OPTIMIZED PERMALINK (ALSO KNOWN AS A "SLUG" IN SEO YOAST)

a. The focused keyword that you are currently uploading content for must be included in the permalink. Do not attempt to automate this process. When you create an automated process, you will start to create duplicate

"Thank you Clay, and the Thrive team. Since implementing the systems you've taught me, we are up over 15% in less than one year."

GUY SHEPHERD

(Founder of Shepherd Automotive Center)

www.ShepherdAutomotive.com

content and Google will penalize you. An example would be: (*Every permalink must be different.*)

Example - www.eitrlounge.com/find-tulsa-mens-haircuts

6.___COMPOSE ANCHOR TEXT FOUND WITHIN YOUR ORIGINAL CONTENT

___You must include your keyword six times within every 1,000 words of your article and you must provide a link from this phrase out to content that relates to it (within your own website, if possible, this is called Intra-linking).

___Wikipedia uses anchor text everywhere. For an example of how they do it, go to wikipedia.org/wiki/Dog. Wikipedia has a hyperlink (to another webpage) that is part the Wikipedia website for the word Canidae, domesticated canid, selectively bred, Eurasia, and other words and phrases.

___When you click each of the phrases, you are taken to another section of Wikipedia's massive library of content. This is what you want on your website. Granted, you may not be as massive as Wikipedia, but you at least want to provide a few links out to related content found within your website. As an example, if you had content that mentioned the city of Orlando, you would either want to provide a link to a portion of your website that discusses the city of Orlando or you would want to provide an link out

to the City of Orlando's website (www.cityoforlando.net).

___Hyperlink out from words related to your keyword

OPTIMIZATION FOCUS to sites of high quality and

integrity (high page rank).

> *Word of Warning: In Google's eyes, who you link to is who you associate yourself with. So be intentional.*

7.___EMBED A VIDEO

___Pages featuring YouTube videos are now ranked higher

in Google search engine results. Remember, Google owns

YouTube. If you were Google, wouldn't you rank websites

that included content found within YouTube higher than

websites that include content found within Vimeo? If you

are using Vimeo for artistic or other reasons, stop using

Vimeo.

___Adding videos to your web pages also increases the

time that each visitor spends on each webpage, which

increases your score.

___Google sincerely cares about the user experience and

they want to reward websites that are able to keep people

engaged and on a website longer. The video should be

embedded right below the text written for it.

1. Go to YouTube
2. On YouTube.com, find a video that you have created to help market your company.
3. On YouTube.com, click the Share button
4. On YouTube.com, click the Embed button
5. On the WordPress-based website, switch from Visual to Text view

NOTABLE QUOTABLE

"Running a startup is like being punched in the face repeatedly. but working for a large company is like being water-boarded. " **- PAUL GRAHAM**

(The co-founder of Y-Combinator, and the coach behind Reddit, Dropbox, AirBnB, etc.)

6. On YouTube.com, select video size: 640 x 360

7. On YouTube.com, copy the iframe embed code.

8. Paste the iframe embed code into the article right below the text written for it. (ie: This content is written for *client name*).

9. On the WordPress-based website, switch back to the Visual tab to verify the video is actually there.

10. On the WordPress-based website,click Update (or Publish if it's a new article).

11. On the WordPress-based website, open "View Article" in a new window to preview your work.

12. On the WordPress-based website, press Play to verify the embedded video works.

8.___NAME ALL IMAGES CORRECTLY

MAKE SURE TO NAME ALL IMAGES BASED UPON YOUR SEARCH ENGINE STRATEGY.

Example - On EITRLounge.com, the images appearing on that page should be labeled "tulsa-mens-haircut-example-1.jpg," and "tulsa-mens-haircut-example-2.jpg."

1. Select a place to put the image.

2. Click on Add Media.

3. Upload the image (must be an original image for each article).

4. Name the title of the image (when you save the image, use dashes, no spaces or underscores)

    example: owasso-mens-haircuts.

5. When you title the image, use the same words, but remove the dashes.

6. Set the image to medium size.

7. Set the image to the left side of the page. Use the formatting buttons to wrap the text around the image.

8. Title the image following this format: Owasso Men's Haircut - Shaving Tools

9. Name the Alt Text: same as the title image. No description of the image is needed.

NOTABLE QUOTABLE

"It takes time, it's a grind. There are no shortcuts. You've got to grind and grind."

- MARK CUBAN

(The iconic billionaire entrepreneur and the owner of the Dallas Mavericks)

"The difference in winning and losing is most often not quitting."

- WALT DISNEY

(The man behind the Disney Empire)

"Timing, perseverance, and ten years of trying will eventually make you look like an overnight success."

- BIZ STONE

(The co-founder of Twitter and Medium.com)

```html
<header class="chapter-title">
        <p>CHAPTER 12</p>

    <h1>
```

FIXING WEBSITE ERRORS

```html
</title>  </h1>
                    <style>
                        #page-background{
                            background-color: #F4B400;
                        }
                            .chapter-title p{
                                text-transform: uppercase;
                                color: white;
                                font-family: 'Proxima Nova ';
                                font-weight: 600;
                            }

                            .chapter-title h1{
                                text-transform: uppercase;
                                color: white;
                                font-family: 'Proxima Nova';
                                font-weight: 900;
                            }
                    </style>
```

FIXING
WEBSITE ERRORS

Here is a list of common website errors you can find by running a website audit from companies like SEMRush.com and how to fix them.

⚠ FIXING SEMRUSH REPORT RELATED ERRORS

___Go to SemRush.com

___Click "Log-In" and use the appropriate user name and password.

___Click the "+" button (located next to Projects).

___Choose a name and domain for the project.

___Click on "Site Audit."

___Crawl all pages and click "Start Edit."

___Click on "Site Audit."

___Click on "View All Issues."

___Once you click "View All Issues." A mountain of errors will appear. This checklist tells you how to fix these errors.

⚠ ALT TAGS

> Example: <img src="wp-content/uploads/image-1.jpg" alt="your image alt text"/>

DIFFICULTY: EASY

___Identify the image(s) missing alt text.

___Use Google Chrome's Developer tools (Keyboard shortcut F12 on PC,⌘⌥I on Mac) to inspect the image.

___Edit the page and select the image missing alt text.

___Click on the pencil icon to edit the image.

___Add text to the "Alt Text" field and click update.

___Update the page to save your changes.

⚠ BROKEN IMAGES

(Best practice is to remove/replace the image.)

DIFFICULTY: EASY

___Locate the broken image.

___Edit the page and select the broken image.

___Click the "Add Media" button and select an image to
    replace the broken one, OR If no appropriate image
    can be added, delete the broken image.

___Update the page.

⚠ DOCTYPE NOT DECLARED

(We recommend you use the Divi builder by ElegantThemes)

DIFFICULTY: HARD

___Verify you are using the Divi theme by ElegantThemes.com.

___Reinstall the Divi theme if already installed

___Go to Appearance > Themes.

___Click on the Divi theme (If active, you must deactivate
    the theme first.)

___Click the "Uninstall" button.

___Once uninstalled, click the "Add New" button at the top
    of the themes page.

___Click the "Upload" button at the top of the themes page

___Upload the latest version of the Divi theme (this will be
    the divi.zip file.)

___Install the theme and activate.

___If the issue persists, contact Elegant Themes or your
    web developer.

⚠ DUPLICATE DESCRIPTION

(See the Meta description steps found in chapter 12, point 3, page 140)

⚠ DUPLICATE TITLES

(Someone copied and pasted.) Change the title to make each unique.
See the Meta Title steps found in chapter 12, point 2 , page 140)

⚠ EXTERNAL LINKS THAT ARE BROKEN

DIFFICULTY: EASY

___Identify the broken link(s) on the page.

___Edit the page.

___Locate the replacement link on the external site

a. Websites occasionally update their links or move content to another location on their site. Websites also remove irrelevant or old content from time to time. See if you can find an updated link before removing the link altogether.

i. Click on the link in your page and click the chain link icon to update the link.

ii. For external links, always check the "Open link in new tab" box.

b. Update the link and the page to save your changes.

c. If no replacement link can be found, remove the link.

⚠ HTTPS ENCRYPTION

DIFFICULTY: MEDIUM

___Purchase an SSL certificate from your website's host (i.e. GoDaddy). Follow your hosting company's instructions for installation. It makes 0% sense to not host your website through GoDaddy.com.

a. For GoDaddy visit godaddy.com/help/install-ssl-certificates-16623.

⚠ INTERNAL LINKS THAT ARE BROKEN

DIFFICULTY: EASY / HARD

EASY - IF YOUR PAGE'S PERMALINK HAS BEEN CHANGED

___Identify the broken link(s).

___Edit the page and select the broken link.

___Update the link to point to a new page or remove the link.

*** Anytime a page is removed from your site, you should create a redirect to a new page using .htaccess rules (301 - permanent redirect or 410 - gone). These rules let Google know where the old page has gone. Use 301 redirects to point an old page to a newer version of the page or a replacement page. ***

HARD - IF YOUR PAGE HAD BEEN PREVIOUSLY

INDEXED BY GOOGLE AND THE PERMALINK CHANGED

**** ___WARNING:___ Incorrectly adding anything to your site's .htaccess file will break your site. We highly recommend you have FTP (File Transfer Protocol) access to your site's server before proceeding. We recommend Filezilla and Cyberduck.

The Syntax - Redirect 301 /old-page/

The first link, '/old-page/', is the relative URL for the page on your website you want to redirect or everything after the .com. The second link, 'https://yoursite.com/new-page/' should be on an absolute URL to the page's new location on the web (where the page should forward to.)

DEFINITION MAGICIAN - **Absolute URL**: A URL including the entire domain. Another way to explain this: Example: https://www.Thrivetimeshow.com/about-us/ **Relative URL**: A URL relative to the domain - does not have the entire domain. Example: /about-us/. Another way to explain this: Example Redirect - Redirect 301 / about-us/ /about

⚠ IMPLEMENTATION -

___Via FTP, open the .htaccess file in the root folder of your WordPress installation.

___Below the line that reads # End WordPress # add a new line and type in your redirect rule (Redirect 301 / your-old-page/ https://yoursite.com/your-new-page/.

___Save and upload the new .htaccess file

___Clear all cache and attempt to go to the URL again. If it redirects to the new page successfully, you're done.

> **a.** If the redirect did not work, verify that all cache has been cleared and that you have the correct old url listed and try again.
>
> **b.** If your site broke after adding the rule, remove the rule completely, save, and re-upload your .htaccess file. Syntax is extremely important. Follow steps 1-3 again until success.
>
> > **Can't find your site's .htaccess file?**
> > .htaccess files are in a group of files known as "dot" files or hidden files. Make sure that in your FTP client you have enabled the ability to view hidden files and it should appear in the same list of files as your "wp-content", "wp-admin" and "wp-includes" folders.

⚠ LOW TEXT TO HTML RATIO

___Write more content to improve the ratio.

⚠ MISSING H1 HEADING

DIFFICULTY: EASY

(Add H1 heading - See chapter 11, part 1, page 131.)

⚠ MISSING ROBOTS.TXT

___Click "Plugins" in the left sidebar.

___Click the "Add New" button at the top.

___In the Search "Plugins" bar, search for: Yoast SEO.

___Click "Install Now" button.

___Click the blue "Activate" link.

___Go to "SEO Tools" Tab.

___Click "Robot.txt" button (this file tells Google which pages it can crawl on your website.)

⚠ MORE THAN ONE H1 HEADING

DIFFICULTY: EASY

___Find which H1 heading can be better used as an H2 heading or is irrelevant.

___Edit the page and change/remove that heading.

⚠ NO FOLLOW ATTRIBUTES

If the links with no-follow attributes link to an external site, this is a best-practice and can be ignored. If the no-follow link is to an internal page follow these steps:

___Locate the link.

___Edit the page and select the link.

___Click on the pencil icon from the link toolbar (displayed when a link is selected.)

___Uncheck the no-follow box & save.

___Update the page.

⚠ PAGE THAT RETURNS 4XX STATUS CODE

___Locate the broken link.

___Delete the link or link it to something that

does exist.

⚠ PAGES THAT CANNOT BE CRAWLED

___Edit the page.

___Go to the Yoast SEO section & click

on the gear icon.

___Change the show in Google searches

dropdown to "index."

⚠ CREATE AN HTML SITEMAP

*(HTML = Humans to See… It MUST be visible! MUST be
referred to as "sitemap" at the bottom of the page.)*

___Go to Pages.

___Click "Add New" button at the top.

___Title it: Sitemap.

___In the right hand column under.

Page Attributes, select "Sitemap" from

Sitemap

Business Coach

- Business Coach
- 1-On-1 Honest Business Assessment
- Business Coach Testimonials
- Need a Business Coach?
  - Is a Business Coach Worthwhile?
  - Rapid Business Growth with a Business Coach
  - The Business Coach Proven System
  - Which Business Coach is Right For You?
  - Why a Business Coach Matters
- Need a Business Coach? Talk with A Business Coach Today!

Business Conferences

- Business Conferences
- Business Conference Testimonials
- Itinerary
- **Business Conferences FAQs**
  - Why You Should Attend One of the Thrivetime Show Business Conferences
  -
  - The Best Business Conferences in 2019
  - 12 Reasons You Should Attend Thrivetime Show Business Conferences

template drop down. If this does not exist

a coder must create an HTML Sitemap.

___Click "Publish."

⚠ INSTALL YOAST SEO

___Log in to WordPress.

___Go to "Plugins."

___Click "Add New."

___Search for Yoast.

___Install and Activate the Plug In.

⚠ CREATE AN .XML SITEMAP

The Yoast plugin will automatically create this for you.

To verify, go to www.yourdomain.com/sitemap_index.xml.

⚠ SUBMIT WEBSITE TO GOOGLE WEBMASTER TOOLS

1. ___Must set up a Gmail account.

2. ___Search for Google Search Console.

3. ___Login with Gmail: www.google.com/webmasters/
    tools/home?hl=en.

4. ___Add a Web Property.

5. ___Paste the URL of the correct website
    (ie: www.eitrlakewood.com) into the field.

6. ___Click the "Continue" button.

7. ___Click on the "HTML Tag Method."

8. ___Copy the metatag below.

9. ___Login to WordPress website.

10. ___Go to Appearance in the left bar.

11. ___Click on "Theme Editor."

12. ___Click Enable Editing.

13. ___Go to Theme Header (header.php) on the right.

14. ___Look for the <head> tag within the theme header.

15. ___Paste the metatag underneath the first <head> tag.

16. ___Click Update File.

17. ___Click on Verify within the Google Search Console

    Occasionally the verification will fail. Verify that you have

    pasted in the meta tag in the correct place, If you have any

    caching plugins active, clear cache. Try to verify again.

18. ___Click Continue.

19. ___Click on the hamburger (3 horizontal line) icon in

    the top left corner.

20. ___Click on the "Address" dropdown, and select

    "Add New Property."

21. ___Paste in the http:// version of your URL

    Example: http://yourdomain.com/.

22. ___Click Done when it finishes verifying

    Repeat Steps 20 - 22 until you have submitted

    each of the following URL versions.

    a. https://yourdomain.com (Only applies if you

    have an SSL certificate installed.)

    b. https://www.yourdomain.com (Only

    applies if you have an SSL certificate installed.)

        c. http://yourdomain.com.

        d. http://www.yourdomain.com.

23. ___Click on "Sitemaps" on the left.

    Type "sitemap_index.xml" at the end of the URL in the right panel where it has your domain.

    Example: https://yourdomain.com/sitemap_index.xml

24. ___In the top bar, paste in your site's full URL

    Example: https://yourdomain.com.

25. ___Once it has verified the page, click "Request Indexing."

26. ___In the top bar, paste in your site's full URL.

    Example: https://yourdomain.com/sitemap/

27. ___Once it has verified the page, click "Request Indexing."

28. ___Click Use Old Version in the bottom-left corner.

29. ___Verify that you are submitting your website for Google to crawl it within the right country preference.

    a.___Click "Search Traffic."

    b.___Click on "International Targeting."

    c.___Click on Country and checkmark targeted servers in the appropriate country.

    d.___Click "Save."

NOTABLE QUOTABLE

"The time will never be just right. You must act now."

- NAPOLEON HILL

(The best-selling author of *Think and Grow Rich* and the man I named by son after. My son's name is Aubrey Napoleon-Hill Clark)

⚠ TOO LOW OF A WORD COUNT

(if you want to dominate Google search engine results you must have at least 1000 words on the page)

___Copy the permalink of the page with not

enough content.

___Record the keywords for this page.

⚠ TOO MUCH TEXT IN THE META DESCRIPTION

___See above (Chapter 12.6, Step 7.)

⚠ TOO MUCH TEXT IN THE META TITLE TAG

___See above (Chapter 12.5, Step.)

⚠ URL TOO LONG (SLUGS AND PERMALINKS)

___Solution: Shorten URL & 301.

"GREAT SPIRITS HAVE ALWAYS ENCOUNTERED
VIOLENT OPPOSITION FROM MEDIOCRE MINDS."
- ALBERT EINSTEIN
DEVELOPER OF THE GENERAL THEORY OF RELATIVITY

CHAPTER 13

OPTIMIZING
YOUTUBE VIDEOS

Why is a Search Engine Optimization Domination Book Talking About YouTube?

 FUN FACT - "YouTube is not simply a website; it is a search engine. YouTube's user-friendliness, combined with the soaring popularity of video content, has made it the second largest search engine behind Google. With 3 billion searches per month, YouTube's search volume is larger than that of Bing, Yahoo, AOL and Ask.com combined." - *Are You Maximizing The Use Of Video In Your Content Marketing Strategy?* - Adam Wagner - Forbes

Marinate on this idea for a moment..."YouTube'S SEARCH VOLUME IS LARGER THAN THAT OF BING, YAHOO, AOL and ASK.com combined!" Think about it like this:

1. Almost every human on the planet uses Google to search for everything that they are looking for.

2. Almost every human on this beautiful planet uses YouTube to search for everything else that they can't find on Google or would prefer to find via a video search engine.

3. Every other search engine DOES NOT MATTER.

YOUTUBE STARTED WITH "JANET'S WARDROBE MALFUNCTION"

We are sure that you were already aware of this, but the good folks who started Google, now own YouTube.com, thus YouTube has become increasingly dominant over time.

YouTube was founded by Chad Hurley, Steven Chen and Jawed Karim who were all early employees at the tech giant, PayPal. Karim claims that the inspiration for starting YouTube came from wanting to see Janet Jackson's wardrobe malfunction and not being able to do so... If you'll remember in 2004, Janet Jackson and Justin Timberlake teamed up to perform during the Super Bowl. During their Super Bowl performance, Janet claimed to have a "Wardrobe malfunction" which caused the world to be exposed to her bare breasts and Jawed Karim wanted to see for himself what happened. But, he couldn't. Why? Because video file sharing was not easy to do at this point in the world's history.

Since that time, Hurley and Chen have said that the original idea behind the creation of YouTube was to create a video version of an online dating service known as Hot or Not. However, the difficulty of finding enough videos related to dating lead the team to change their plans and to begin accepting the uploads of nearly any type of video.

THE DOMAIN FOR WWW.YOUTUBE.COM OFFICIALLY LAUNCHED ON FEBRUARY 14TH OF 2005, AND WAS PURCHASED BY GOOGLE FOR OVER $1 BILLION JUST 1 YEAR LATER

YouTube was founded as a venture capital-funded technology business, receiving a $11.5 million investment from the legendary venture capital fund, Sequoia Capital and an additional $8 million of funding from Artis Capital Management between November of 2005 and April of 2006. YouTube was originally founded and located above a pizzeria and Japanese restaurant located in San Mateo, California.

In July of 2006, YouTube announced that they were receiving more than 65,000 new videos to upload every day and that YouTube.com was experiencing over 100 million views each and every day. By May of 2011, nearly 48 hours of content were now being uploaded to the website every minute.

ON OCTOBER 9TH, 2006 GOOGLE, INC. ACQUIRED YOUTUBE FOR $1.65 BILLION IN GOOGLE STOCK

Although most people on the planet, did not get excited, worried or emotionally involved in this transaction in any way, shape or form, we did. The profundity of the world's largest search engine buying the world's largest video search engine BLEW OUR MINDs and we have been CLOSELY watching the integration of the two brands closely ever since. Consider this...

- On February 28th, 2017, YouTube announced the launch of YouTube TV, a subscription service that would only be available to United States customers in New York City, Los Angeles, Chicago, Philadelphia and San Francisco for $35 per month. This service provided users with live streams of programming from the five major broadcast networks (NBC, Fox, The CW, CBS, and ABC) as well as access to the 40 cable channels that were at the time owned by the five major networks (The Walt Disney Company,

CBS Corporation, 21st Century Fox, NBCUniversal and Turner Broadcasting System, Bravo, USA Network, Disney Channel, CNN, Cartoon Network, E!, Fox Sports, FX and ESPN) all for just $35 per month.   Why would you continue to pay your current cable company or satellite dish company over $100 per month to watch the same programming that you can now watch for just $35 per month? You wouldn't and people are cancelling their cable and satellite TV subscriptions in droves.

- In January of 2019, YouTube rolled out its $40-a-month-service which was made available in 95 new U.S. markets, to cover a total of 195 regions or approximately 98% of American households. YouTube TV included the live streaming of more than 60 networks including CNN, ABC and Fox. According to a story put out by CNBC titled, YouTube's bet against big cable announces nationwide expansion, "YouTube TV is reportedly losing money on every subscriber." **YouTube TV is 100% focused on convincing you to switch from cable and satellite services even if it involves losing money on every subscriber.**

- As of June 30th of 2019, YouTube TV is showcasing its most aggressive no-brainer offer yet: "Cable-free live TV is here - Live TV from 70+ networks. Local sports and news. No cable box required. TRY IT FREE. $49.99 per month. Cancel anytime." Think about that for a second...with YouTube TV you gain access to 6 accounts per household, everyone gets their own login and you receive notifications when your show is on, all for just $49.99 per month. With

YouTube TV, their cloud DVR (Digital Video Recorder) provides you with unlimited storage space and you can stream your library wherever you go. Unless you have hurt your cranium in a severe accident, YouTube TV would appear to be the biggest no-brainer offer of all time, and it is. In addition, YouTube is aggressively growing he number of streaming movies that it has made available to YouTube subscribers. In the not-so-distant-future YouTube will be the place that you go to watch the TV shows and movies that you know and the concept of cable television and satellite TV will be remembered with the same reverence that we all have for Blockbuster Video (may Blockbuster rest in peace).

DOMINATING THE SEARCH RESULTS OF THE SECOND MOST TRAFFICKED WEBSITE IS NOT A BAD THING:

YouTube is the second biggest search engine and the second most trafficked website in the world! In fact, according to *Business Insider*, there are 400 HOURS of videos uploaded to YouTube every single minute and the *Wall Street Journal* reports over 1 billion hours of videos are watched each day on YouTube.

Since, this is a book about Search Engine Domination, we will choose to stick with the theme and the focus of search engine optimization, but the point is that there are a TON of people searching on YouTube, and more people are joining the YouTube TV band wagon each and every day.

IF YOU ARE GOOGLE SEARCHING SOMETHING, SOON YOU WILL COME IN CONTACT WITH YOUTUBE'S SEARCH RESULTS:

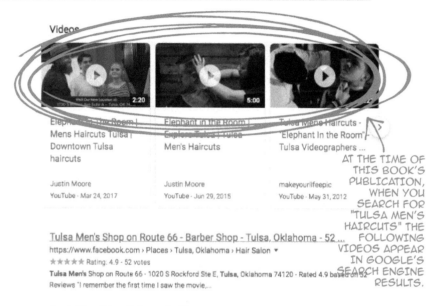

AT THE TIME OF THIS BOOK'S PUBLICATION, WHEN YOU SEARCH FOR "TULSA MEN'S HAIRCUTS" THE FOLLOWING VIDEOS APPEAR IN GOOGLE'S SEARCH ENGINE RESULTS.

Uploading a video to YouTube is pretty straightforward, but in order to make sure you get the most search engine "love" from Google and YouTube, you need to make sure that you are acting based upon the following YouTube Search Engine Optimization Laws.

YouTube Search Engine Optimization Laws

THE PERSON WITH THE MOST RELEVANT CONTENT WINS.

Regardless of who is the best (from your perspective), the YouTube content creator who most consistently produces the most content and the highest quality content will always be ranked at the top of the YouTube search engine results. Google / YouTube wants to only rank the best and most relevant content at the top of their search engine results. Why? Because we would quickly stop using YouTube if every video that came up at the top of their search engine results was 100% terrible, nonsensical, not consistent, sketchy and scammy. Thus, if you want to rank high in YouTube search engine results it is imperative that you consistently produce high quality and relevant content. What makes high quality content? You want to make videos that actually make sense and that YOU actually took the time to write an outline for. We will use an incredible client by the name of Josh Spurrell, who lives in Edmonton, Canada. He is Canada's version of an American certified public accountant and he is now the highest rated, most reviewed and most search engine optimized accountant in all of Canada. Why? Because he has chosen to consistently produce original, relevant and high-quality content.

NEVER LET A VIDEO GET PUBLISHED WITHOUT IT BEING FULLY OPTIMIZED.

a. YouTube is known for judging and ranking (or not ranking) your videos at a lightening fast pace so do not upload a video and publish it with plans to come back later and change all of the optimization. You must optimize your video as you upload it to YouTube.com.

Bonus Note - Save your video as the keyword (separated by hyphens) you are going for before uploading to YouTube

Tuscaloosa churches

FILTER

July 7, 2019; First Presbyterian Church, Tuscaloosa, Alabama
FPC Tuscaloosa · 5 views · Streamed 4 days ago

First Presbyterian Church; Tuscaloosa, Alabama; July 7, 2019 Serving Christ from the Heart of Tuscaloosa www.fpctusc.org Music ...

New

June 30, 2019; First Presbyterian Church, Tuscaloosa, Alabama
FPC Tuscaloosa · 6 views · Streamed 1 week ago

First Presbyterian Church; Tuscaloosa, Alabama; June 30, 2019 Serving Christ from the Heart of Tuscaloosa www.fpctusc.org ...

New

OPTIMIZE YOUR TITLE

a. Make sure your video Title Tag is as least 5 words long and that it includes the keyword you are trying to optimize for, as well as be attention-grabbing. If you create the best content that the planet has ever seen and you name it incorrectly, nobody will EVER find it. Thus, you must be very intentional about how you name your videos. As an example, if you want your videos to come up TOP in the Google search engine results for the keyword phrase, "Owensboro Church" you would need to title your videos "Owensboro Church | God's Plan for Your Life."

b. Just like with Google search engine optimization, you must also create original content each and every time you upload a video. Are we saying that every title tag must be slightly different? Yes. Are we saying that every video description must be different? Yes. Are we saying that you cannot just copy and paste the descriptions of each and every video? Yes.

Owensboro Church | God's Plan for Your Life.

Q All Images News Maps Videos More   Settings Tools

About 5,780 results (0.28 seconds)

YOUTUBE TITLE TAG

Owensboro Church | God's Plan for Your Life - YouTube
https://www.youtube.com/watch?v=ftRlvWVdjSw_c

Mar 28, 2019 - Uploaded by HIS Church Owensboro
Are you looking for an **Owensboro Church** you can believe in? During this episode of the **HIS Church** Podcast ...

Owensboro Church | - YouTube
https://www.youtube.com/watch?v=ftRlvWVdjSw

YOUTUBE DESCRIPTION

Apr 25, 2019 - Uploaded by HIS Church Owensboro
Are you looking for an **Owensboro Church** you can believe in? During this episode of **the HIS Church** Youtube ...

YOU MUST CREATE COMPELLING CONTENT THAT PEOPLE ACTUALLY WATCH.

a. You might be asking, what is the magical formula for creating compelling content that people will actually watch? In order to create content that the human race will actually want to watch, you MUST create content using the following formula that we have developed over the years:

i. Write a Pithy, Clicky and Sticky Headline That People Simply Cannot Keep Themselves from Clicking.
This just in...humans on the planet earth cannot stop themselves from clicking headlines involving:

1. Scandals
2. Celebrities
3. Controversial World-Views
4. Top 10 Lists
5. How To...

ii. Support this headline with facts that are verifiable.

1. Support this headline with notable quotables that were once said or written by somebody with more credibility than yourself (Steve Jobs, Walt Disney, Jesus, Socrates, etc.).

iii. Support this headline with a STORY that is true that demonstrates the practicality of what you are saying.

iv. Leave your viewers with a CALL TO ACTION that is doable, practical and realistic.

v. Tell your viewers what they can expect to find on the next episode of the content that you are producing

UPLOAD A CUSTOM THUMBNAIL

a. Simply put, thumbnails are what gets clicked and the more of your videos that gets clicked and watched, the better your video will be ranked and received.

OPTIMIZE YOUR DESCRIPTION

a. Make sure that you fill this section out and write more than a sentence or two. Make sure to add a link back to your website, a call to action, and more information about the video. if you wanted to properly optimize your videos to be indexed / ranked at the very highest YouTube ranking you would want to make sure that you optimize your YouTube descriptions properly. In your YouTube descriptions you want to make sure that you include:

   i. The keyword phrase that you are trying to optimize for.

   ii. A backlink to your website.

   iii. Your phone number.

iv. Relevant content that clearly relates to the keyword phrase that you are trying to optimize your content for.

YOUTUBE DESCRIPTION

YOUTUBE KEYWORDS & TAGS

ADD THE "KEYWORDS" AND "TAGS" THAT YOUR IDEAL AND LIKELY BUYERS ARE SEARCHING FOR THE MOST. ADD THE TRANSCRIPT/CAPTIONS

a. YouTube will do this for you automatically and it actually is considered in your rankings however since they are automatically generated, the quality is not great so you will want to be okay with errors or edit them yourself.

Not only is YouTube already the second largest search engine in the world, but it is only going to get bigger over time as more and more people choose to use YouTube.TV instead of cable and satellite TV. Optimizing your content to show up at the top of the YouTube search results will become increasingly important. You and your business simply cannot wait to figure out how YouTube optimization works.

```
<header class="chapter-title">
        <p>CHAPTER 14</p>
        <h1>
```

IT'S TIME TO GET ON YOUR GRIND

```
        </h1>
</header>


            <style>
                #page-background{
                    background-color: #0F9D58;
                }

                    .chapter-title h1{
                        text-transform: uppercase;
                        color: white;
                        font-family: 'Proxima Nova';
                        font-weight: 900;
                    }
                </style>
```

NOTABLE QUOTABLE

"He becometh poor that dealeth with a slack hand: but the hand of the diligent maketh rich."

- PROVERBS 10:4

(The Holy Bible)

CONCLUSION: IT'S TIME TO GET ON YOUR GRIND

Alright, now that you know how search engines work, it's time for you to do something about it. The way we see it, you have 5 options to choose from:

1. Immediately start implementing what you've learned because you know what to do and you now have both the technology and the drive needed to succeed.

2. Immediately, read this book again. Why? Repetition is how you learn and thus just the act of reading this book again will help you to better understand what you need to do.

3. Immediately, have our marketing firm, the MYLE (Make Your life Epic) Agency analyze your website to show you what's wrong with it and what you can do about it by filling out the form at www.ThrivetimeShow.com/Website

4. Immediately, book your ticket to attend our next in-person workshop at the 20,000 square foot facility in Tulsa, Oklahoma for the low, low price of $37 per ticket because you are the owner of this powerful, potentially life-changing book. We do keep the attendance limited so you wont find yourself in an audience filled with thousands of people, thus you can actually ask questions and get them answered.

    To claim your tickets, email the following information to us:

Name: _____

Phone: _____

Email: _____

Business Name: _____

5. You can hire a reputable search engine optimization firm of which we can proudly recommend 3 firms and only 3 firms based upon our experience having personally worked with hundreds of search engine firms, marketing firms, and so-called internet marketing and digital advertising experts:

> **01. BRUCECLAY.COM** - Bruce is considered to be the "Father of Search Engine Optimization." Clay and I have paid Bruce thousands of dollars throughout the years and it has been worth every penny of it. In fact, Clay has actually had him on our chart-topping ThrivetimeShow.com podcast as a guest. Throughout Bruce's legendary career he has worked on projects for Coldwell Banker, L.L. Bean, NEC, Century 21, etc. He is the best-selling author of *Search Engine Optimization All-In-One for Dummies (9 books in 1) and Content Marketing - Strategies for Professionals.*
>
> **02. SEOINC.COM** - For more than 19 years Garry Grant's company SEOInc.com has been one of the leading search engine optimization firms on the planet. Throughout Garry's historic career his firm has been the search engine optimization company of choice for massive companies who have the money to hire any firm that they want. His current and past client list includes: SC Johnson, Sandals, 20th Century Fox, OXI Fresh Carpet Cleaning, Wedding Wire, etc.

179

Garry is a high-energy guy who truly is passionate about helping his clients to DOMINATE the search engine results. Garry's interview on the *Thrivetime Show* Podcast was a favorite of our listeners.

03. MYLEAGENCY.COM

- En route to starting and growing DJConnection.com, EITRLounge.com, EpicPhotos.com, and multiple other ventures Clay could never find a turn-key marketing firm that could provide search engine optimization, graphic design, photography, videography, content writing, advertisement writing, sales scripting, social media marketing, digital ad management and strategy coaching all in-house, in one place and on a month-to-month basis, so he built his own firm. We are proud to recommend ourselves, but don't take our word for it. Search for "Clay Clark reviews" on Google or "Clay Clark reviews" in YouTube and you will quickly find literally thousands of reviews from great people like you whose businesses we've been able to dramatically grow in part because of Search Engine Domination.

What Should You Look for Before Hiring a Search Engine Optimization Firm:

1. Verifiable references from real clients who have really experienced tangible results and not just fabulous feelings.

2. Verifiable video reviews from real clients who have been really satisfied with the real experience they really had with the search engine firm.

3. A history of success. When possible avoid startup search engine marketing firms. We have heard thousands of sob and horror stories from great people like you that we have met at in-person workshops who can no longer get a hold of their "search engine expert" who is now "ghosting them" or who can't find their passwords.

WARNING: MOST PEOPLE ARE 100% WRONG ABOUT NEARLY EVERYTHING ON THE PLANET EARTH AND THAT INCLUDES SEARCH ENGINES.

FUN FACT – "78 percent of the men interviewed had cheated on their current partner."
- WASHINGTONPOST.COM

FUN FACT – "75% of employees steal from the workplace and most do so repeatedly." **- CBSNEWS.COM**

FUN FACT - "75% of Job Applicants Lie on Resumes." **- CNBC.COM**

NOTABLE QUOTABLE

"In the future, the great division will be between those who have trained themselves to handle these complexities and those who are overwhelmed by them -- those who can acquire skills and discipline their minds and those who are irrevocably distracted by all the media around them and can never focus enough to learn."

- Robert Greene
(The best-selling author of *Mastery*)

"The way to get started is to quit talking and begin doing."

- WALT DISNEY

(The iconic entrepreneur and the
co-founder of the Walt Disney Empire)

WANT TO LEARN MORE SO THAT YOU CAN EARN MORE?

THROUGHOUT THE YEARS CLAY HAS
WRITTEN THE FOLLOWING BOOKS.

START HERE
The World's Best Business Growth & Consulting Book: Business Growth Strategies from the World's Best Business Coach

DON'T LET YOUR EMPLOYEES HOLD YOU HOSTAGE
This candid book shares how to avoid being held hostage by employees.

F6 JOURNAL
Meta Thrive Time Journal

THE ENTREPRENEUR'S DRAGON ENERGY
The Mindset Kanye, Trump and You Need to Succeed

BOOM
The 13 Proven Steps to Business Success

MAKE YOUR LIFE EPIC
Clay shares his journey and struggle from the dorm room to the board room during his raw and action-packed story of how he built DJConnection.com.

JACKASSARY
Jackassery will serve as a beacon of light for other entrepreneurs that are looking to avoid troublesome employees and difficult situations. This is real. This is raw. This is unfiltered entrepreneurship.

THE ART OF GETTING THINGS DONE
Clay Clark breaks down the proven, time-tested and time freedom creating super moves that you can use to create both the time freedom and financial freedom that most people only dream about.

THRIVE
How to Take Control of Your Destiny and Move Beyond Surviving... Now!

WILL NOT WORK FOR FOOD
9 Big Ideas for Effectively Managing Your Business in an Increasingly Dumb, Distracted & Dishonest America

WHEEL OF WEALTH
An Entrepreneur's Action Guide

BECOMING THE ELEPHANT IN THE ROOM
57 Words of Wisdom and Mindsets to Becoming a Successful Person

Experience Business School without the B.S., listen to the Thrivetime Show Podcast featuring the following guests and more:

 MICHAEL LEVINE - The public relations consultant of choice for Nike, Prince, Michael Jackson, President Clinton and Charlton Heston.

WOLFGANG PUCK - The man whose name has become synonymous with fine dining and gourmet cuisine.

 DAVID ROBINSON - The NBA Hall of Fame basketball player, turned successful investor and entrepreneur.

SCOTT BELSKY - The founder of Behance and the Chief Product Officer and Executive Vice President of Adobe.

 JOHN MAXWELL - The 8x *New York Times* best-selling author and leadership expert.

GUY KAWASAKI - The legendary former key Apple employee turned venture capitalist, best-selling author, and Mercedes product ambassador.

 SHARON LECHTER - The *New York Times* Best-Selling Co-Author of *Rich Dad Poor Dad*.

PASTOR CRAIG GROESCHEL - The senior pastor of the largest Protestant church in America, with over 100,000 weekly attendees (Lifechurch.tv).

"You guys are brilliant, entertaining, and crushing it."
- CRAIG GROECHEL
(The pastor of the largest Protestant church in America)

....

"This has been thrilling!"

- SETH GODIN

*(Best-selling author of 18 books and the former
Yahoo! Vice President of marketing)*

....

 DAVID BACH - One of America's most trusted financial experts who has written nine consecutive *New York Times* bestsellers with 7 million+ books in print.

ZACK O'MALLEY GREENBURG - The senior editor for *Forbes* and 3x best-selling author of *3 Kings: Diddy, Dre, Jay-Z, and Hip Hop's Multibillion-Dollar Rise*, *Empire State of Mind: How Jay-Z Went from Street Corner to Corner Office*, and *Michael Jackson, Inc.: The Rise, Fall, and Rebirth of a Billion-Dollar Empire*.

 JOHN LEE DUMAS - The most downloaded entrepreneur-focused business podcaster of all-time (EOFire.com),

SETH GODIN - *New York Times* best-selling author of *Purple Cow*, and former Yahoo! Vice President of marketing.

 DAN HEATH - *New York Times* best-selling author of *Made to Stick*, and Duke University professor.

LEE COCKERELL - The former Executive Vice President of Walt Disney World who once managed 40,000 employees, and 1,000,000 guests per week.

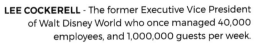 **BEN SHAPIRO** - Conservative talk pundit, *Fox News* contributor, political commentator, and best-selling Author.

See additional guests at **ThrivetimeShow.com**